mustsees

HAWAIIAN ISLANDS

Belongs to.
Charm &
Dave

Editorial Director	Cynthia Clayton Ochterbeck

mustsees Hawaiian Islands

Editor	Alison Coupe
Principal Writer	Diane Bair, Pamela Wright
Production Manager	Natasha G. George
Cartography	Peter Wrenn
Photo Editor	Yoshimi Kanazawa
Photo Research	Jenni Rainford
Proofreaders	Jonathan P. Gilbert, Rachel Mills
Layout	John Higginbottom, Natasha G. George
Cover & Interior Design	Chris Bell

Contact Us:	Michelin Maps and Guides
	One Parkway South
	Greenville, SC 29615
	USA
	www.michelintravel.com
	michelin.guides@us.michelin.com
	Michelin Maps and Guides
	Hannay House
	39 Clarendon Road
	Watford, Herts WD17 1JA
	UK
	☎(01923) 205 240
	www.ViaMichelin.com
	travelpubsales@uk.michelin.com

Special Sales:	For information regarding bulk sales, customized editions and premium sales, please contact our Customer Service Departments:

USA	1-800-432-6277
UK	(01923) 205 240
Canada	1-800-361-8236

Michelin Apa Publications Ltd

A joint venture between Michelin and Langenscheidt

58 Borough High Street, London SE1 1XF, United Kingdom

© 2009 Michelin Apa Publications Ltd
ISBN 978-1-906261-58-0
Printed: December 2008
Printed and bound: Himmer, Germany

Note to the reader:

While every effort is made to ensure that all information printed in this guide is correct and up-to-date, Michelin Apa Publications Ltd. accepts no liability for any direct, indirect or consequential losses howsoever caused so far as such can be excluded by law. Admission prices listed for sights in this guide are for a single adult, unless otherwise specified.

Welcome to the Hawaiian Islands

Ka Makani O Kihei

Hoku Welu Welu

Lele Wale Aku La

p 104

p 155

TABLE OF CONTENTS

★★★ ATTRACTIONS

Unmissable attractions awarded three stars in this guide include:

Volcanoes National Park, Hawaii p 29

Bishops Museum and Planetarium, Oahu p 119

Na Pali Coast, Kauai p 85

Kaunaoa Beach, Hawaii p 26

MUST KNOW

©Linda Bair/Dreamstime.com

Hana Highway, Maui p 65

©Andre Nantel/iStockphoto.com

USS Arizona Memorial,
Pearl Harbor, Oahu p 125

Hawaii Tourism Japan

Hulopoe Beach, Lanai p 147

©Gavin James/Bigstockphoto.com

Kalalau Hiking Trail, Kauai p 85

©Ron Chapple Stock/Fotolia.com

Haleakala National
Park, Maui p 62

STAR ATTRACTIONS

★★★ ATTRACTIONS

Unmissable Hawaiian Islands sights

For more than 75 years people have used the Michelin stars to take the guesswork out of travel. Our star-rating system helps you make the best decisions on where to go, what to do, and what to see.

★★★	Absolutely Must See
★★	Really Must See
★	Must See
No Star	See

ACTIVITIES
Look for the Michelin Man to find out about the top activities on Hawaiian Islands.

Entertainment
Barefoot Bar at Duke's (OAH) *141*
Germaine's Luau (OAH) *142*
Palace Theater (HAW) *54*

Botanical Gardens
Koko Crater BG (OAH) *117*
Kula BG (MAU) *67*

Kids
Children's Discovery
   Center (OAH) *136*
Puukohola Heiau NHS (HAW) *46*

Recreation
Relaxing at "From Here to
   Eternity Beach" (OAH) *111*
Surfing at Maalaea Harbor (MAU) *71*
Surfing at Hookipa Beach (MAU) *61*

Restaurants
Giovanni's Shrimp (OAH) *111*
Island Lava Java (HAW) *167*
Kualapuu Cook House *176*

Shopping
Hilo Farmers' Market (HAW) *53*
Lahaina (MAU) *74*

Spas
SpaHalekulani (OAH) *143*
Spa Without Walls (HAW) *55*

Tours
Biking down a Volcano (MAU) *68*
Helicopter Tours (Niihau) *163*

Remember to look out for the Michelin Man for top activities.

STAR ATTRACTIONS

CALENDAR OF EVENTS

Listed below is a selection of Hawaii's most popular annual events. Please note that the dates may change from year to year. For more information, contact the Hawaii Visitors and Convention Bureau **(808-923-1811; www.gohawaii.com)**.

January
Hula Bowl
800-971-1232
Aloha Stadium, Honolulu, Oahu
www.hulabowlhawaii.com

February
Lunar New Year
808-521-4934
Chinatown, Honolulu, Oahu
www.chinatownhi.com
Waimea Town Celebration
808-338-1332
Waimea, Kauai
www.wkbpa.org
Pro Bowl
808-486-9300
Aloha Stadium, Honolulu, Oahu
www.nfl.com

March
Celebration of the Arts
808-669-6200
Ritz-Carlton, Kapalua, Maui
Prince Kuhio Celebration of the Arts
808-240-6369
Grand Hyatt Kauai Resort,
Poipu Beach, Kauai
www.poipubeach.org

April
Merrie Monarch Festival
808-935-9168
Hilo Civic Center, Hilo,
Big Island (week after Easter)
www.merriemonarchfestival.org

May
International Festival of Canoes
808-667-9175
Lahaina, Maui
www.mauifestivalofcanoes.com
Kona Chocolate Festival
808-640-5500
Kailua-Kona, Big Island
www.konachocolatefestival.com
Molokai Ka Hula Piko Hula Festival
808-553-3876
Papohaku Beach Park, Molokai
www.molokaievents.com

June
King Kamehameha Celebration
808-586-0333
All islands
www.hawaii.gov/dags/king_kamehameha_commission
Maui Film Festival at Wailea
808-572-FILM
Wailea, Maui
www.mauifilmfestival.com

July
Hawaii International Jazz Festival
808-941-9974
Oahu and Maui
www.hawaiijazz.com
Parker Ranch Rodeo
808-885-5898
Parker Ranch, Waimea,
Big Island
www.parkerranch.com

MUST KNOW

Ukulele Festival
808-732-3739
Kapiolani Park
Waikiki, Oahu
www.roysakuma.net

August
Establishment Day Festival
808-882-7218
Puukohola Heiau Historic Site
Kawaihae, Big Island
Hawaiian International Billfish Tournament
Kailua-Kona, Big Island
808-329-6155
www.hibtfishing.com
Honolulu Family Festival
808-924-1907
Ala Moana Beach Park,
Honolulu, Oahu
www.honolulufamilyfestival.com
Puuhonua O Honaunau Festival
808-328-2326
Puuhonua O Honaunau National
Historical Park, Big Island
www.nps.gov/puho

September
Aloha Festivals
800-589-1771
All islands
www.alohafestivals.com
Hawaii International Film Festival
808-528-3457
All islands
www.hiff.org
Na Wahine O Ke Kai Molokai to Oahu Canoe Race
808-259-7112
Hale O Lono Harbor, Molokai
www.nawahineokekai.com
Mauifest Hawaii
808-573-5530
Maui Arts & Cultural Center
Hotel Hana-Maui, Hana
www.mauifest.net

October
Ironman Triathlon World Championship
Kailua-Kona, Big Island
808-329-0063
www.ironmanlive.com
Molokai Hoe Canoe Race
808-259-7112
Hale o Lono, Molokai
www.OHCRA.com

November
Grand Slam
800-742-8258
Poipu Bay Resort Golf Course,
Kauai
www.pga.com
Invitational Wreath Exhibit
808-967-8222
Hawaii Volcanoes National Park,
Big Island
www.volcanoartcenter.org
VANS Triple Crown Surfing Championships
North shore of Oahu
www.triplecrownofsurfing.com
(Nov–Dec)
World Invitational Hula Festival
808-735-7950
Waikiki Shell, Honolulu, Oahu
www.worldhula.com

December
Anniversary Commemoration Pearl Harbor
USS Arizona Memorial
808-422-0561
Honolulu, Oahu
www.arizonamemorial.org
Honolulu Marathon
808-734-7200
Honolulu, Oahu
www.honolulumarathon.org
Waimea Christmas Parade and Festival
808-937-2833
Waimea, Big Island

CALENDAR OF EVENTS

PRACTICAL INFORMATION

MUST KNOW

WHEN TO GO

There is no bad time to travel to the Hawaiian Islands. The busiest time is from mid-December through March, when mainlanders rush to the islands to cure their winter blues. Generally, you'll find the best lodging discounts from late September to mid-December. **Weather** is consistently warm throughout the year, with nighttime temperatures ranging about 10 degrees lower than during the day. The average water temperature is 74°F (23.3°C), with a summer high of 80°F (26.7°C). That said, you'll find diverse environments on each of the islands, from misty tropical rain forests, cool mountaintops, arid deserts and sunny beaches—all within a few short miles of each other. The major difference between winter (Nov–Apr) and summer (May–Oct) is the surf.

You'll find the biggest waves during the winter months, the most popular time for surfers to head to Hawaiian beaches. The **wettest months** are from November through March; most of the rain falls in the mountains and valleys on the windward (northeastern) side of the islands.

What to Pack

Casual is the rule here, but if you plan to dine in high-end restaurants, pack dressy resort wear. Bring a rain jacket and a sweater; it's cooler in the high country, and sudden showers are common. No need to bring big sports gear, like surfboards; rentals are available.

KNOW BEFORE YOU GO

Before you go, contact the following organizations to obtain maps and information about sight-seeing, accommodations, travel packages, recreational opportunities and seasonal events.

Hawaii Visitors and Convention Bureau (HCVB)
2270 Kalakaua Ave., Suite 801, Honolulu (Oahu), HI 96815
800-464-2924
www.gohawaii.com

Big Island Visitors Bureau/Hilo
250 Keawe St., Hilo, HI 96720
808-961-5797
www.bigisland.org

Big Island Visitors Bureau/ Waikoloa
250 Waikoloa Beach Dr., Waikoloa, HI 96738
808-886-1655
www.bigisland.org

Kauai Visitors and Convention Bureau
4334 Rice St, Suite 101, Lihue, HI 96766
800-262-1400; 808-245-3971
www.kauaidiscovery.com

Destination Lanai
431 Seventh St., Suite A, Lanai City, HI 96763
800-947-4774
www.visitlanai.net

Maui Visitors Bureau
1727 Wili Pa Loop, Wailuku, HI 96793
800-525-6284
www.visitmaui.com

Molokai Visitors Association
2 Kamoi St., Suite 200, Kaunakakai, HI 96748
808-553-3876; 800-800-6367
www.molokai-hawaii.com

Seasonal Temperatures in Hawaii			
	Jan	Apr	July	Oct
Avg. high	79°F/26°C	82°F/28.9°C	88°F/31°C	87°F/30.6°C
Avg. low	64°F/17.8°C	66°F/18.9°C	70°F/21°C	69°F/20.6°C

Oahu Visitors Bureau
733 Bishop St., Suite 1520,
Honolulu, HI 96813
808-524-0722
www.visit-oahu.com

INTERNATIONAL VISITORS

Visitors from outside the US can obtain information from the Hawaii Visitors and Convention Bureau on Oahu (*2270 Kalakaua Ave., Suite 801, Honolulu; 808-924-0246; www.gohawaii.com*) or from the US embassy or consulate in their country of residence. For a complete list of American consulates and embassies abroad, visit the US State Department Bureau of Consular Affairs listing on the internet at *http://travel.state.gov/links.html*.

Entry Requirements

Travelers entering the United States under the **Visa Waiver Program (VWP)** must have a **machine-readable passport**. Any traveler without a machine-readable passport will be required to obtain a visa before entering the US. Citizens of VWP countries are permitted to enter the US for general business or tourist purposes for a maximum of 90 days without needing a visa. Requirements for the Visa Waiver Program can be found at the Department of State's Visa Services website: http://travel.state.gov/vwp.html.

All citizens of non-participating countries must have a visitor's visa. Upon entry, non-resident foreign visitors must present a valid passport and round-trip transportation ticket. Naturalized Canadian citizens should carry their citizenship papers.

US Customs

All articles brought into the US must be declared at the time of entry. Prohibited items: plant material; firearms and ammunition (if not for sporting purposes); meat or poultry products. For more information, contact the **US Customs Service** (*1300 Pennsylvania Ave. NW, Washington, DC 20229; 202-354-1000; www.cbp.gov*) or the **Hawaii Department of Agriculture** (*808-973-9560; www.hawaiiag.org*).

Because rabies doesn't exist in Hawaii, all animals entering Hawaii must be held for four months at the quarantine facility on Oahu. Hawaiian officials won't let you enter with live plants, animals, fresh fruits or vegetables of any kind. Due to restrictions on taking fruits, plants and animals out of Hawaii, all baggage bound from Hawaii to the US mainland is subject to pre-flight inspection by the US Department of Agriculture. You can bring only pre-packed and pre-inspected fruits to the US mainland.

PRACTICAL INFORMATION

GETTING THERE

By Air

Honolulu International Airport (HNL), on **Oahu**, located about 3 miles west of downtown Honolulu, is where the majority of visitors to the Hawaiian Islands land *(808-836-6411; www.honolu luairport.com)*. From here, you can hop on flights to the other major islands *(see opposite)*. Maui's Kahului Airport is also seeing more direct traffic from the mainland.

Airport Waikiki Shuttle provides 24-hour transportation from the airport to any hotel in Waikiki for $15 round-trip.

TheBus *(see p16)* runs from the airport to major stops in Waikiki Beach and downtown Honolulu. Taxis and rental-cars *(see p16)* are available at Honolulu International and at all the airports listed below.

Big Island – Hilo International Airport (ITO) is located 2 miles east of Hilo on the Big Island's eastern shore *(808-934-5840; www6.hawaii.gov/dot/airports/ hawaii/ito)*. There is no public bus service from the airport, and hotel shuttles are limited.

Important Numbers	
Emergency (Police/Ambulance/Fire Department, 24hrs)	**911**
Police (non-emergency, Mon–Fri 9am–6pm)	
Honolulu Police	808-529-3111
Kauai Police	808-241-1653
Big Island	808-326-4646 (Hilo) 808-961-2213
Maui and Lanai	808-244-6300
Poison Control	800-222-1222
Medical Referral:	
Queen's Medical Center Referral Program, Oahu	808-547-4606 or 800-342-5901, ext. 4606
Hilo Medical Center, Big Island	808-974-4700
Maui Memorial Hospital, Maui	808-244-9056
Lihue Wilcox Memorial, Kauai	808-245-1010
Lanai Community Hospital, Lanai	808-565-6411
Dental Emergencies: Dental Hotline	(Oahu) 808-944-8863
24-hour Pharmacies: Long's Drugs in downtown Honolulu	
1330 Pali Hwy.	808-536-7302
2220 S. King St.	808-949-4781
Coast Guard Search and Rescue	800-552-6458
To report an injured turtle, dolphin or whale	800-853-1964

MUST KNOW

Twenty **cab companies** operate on the Big Island and fares are not cheap. Once you're in town, use the **Hele-On** ("Let's Go") bus to get around the island—it's free.

Kona International Airport (KOA) at Keahole is located about 7 miles northwest of Kailua-Kona *(808-329-3423; www6.hawaii. gov/dot/airports/hawaii/koa)*. **SpeediShuttle** *(877-242-5777; www.speedishuttle.com)* offers service to Big Island resorts. (Also serves Maui, Kauai, and Oahu.)

Maui – Kahului Airport (OGG) is located on the northern edge of the land bridge between Haleakala and the West Maui Mountain Range on Maui *(808-872-3893, www6.hawaii.gov/dot/airports/ maui/ogg)*. **SpeediShuttle** *(above)* and **Maui Shuttle** *(808-669-2300; www.mauishuttle.com)* offer shuttle services from the airport to resorts.

Kauai – Lihue Airport (LIH) is located about 1.5 miles east of Lihue, on the southeast coast of Kauai *(808-246-1448; www6. hawaii.gov/dot/airports/kauai/lih)*. **SpeediShuttle** *(above)* offers services from the airport. Bus service on the island is limited, so many visitors use rental cars to get around.

Lanai – Tiny **Lanai Airport (LNY)** is located about 3 miles southwest of Lanai City *(808-836-6417; www6. hawaii.gov/dot/airports/lanai/lny)*. Its single runway serves primarily scheduled interisland and commuter traffic. The two major resorts on the island provide shuttle service from the airport.

Molokai – Molokai Airport (MKK) is located about 4 miles

west of Kualapuu on Maunaloa Highway *(808-567-6361; www6. hawaii.gov/dot/airports/molokai/ mkk)*. The airport has two runways that accommodate commuter/air taxi and general interisland flights.

By Cruise Boat

Cruises have become a popular way to see the Hawaiian Islands. Most cruises begin and end in Honolulu, but longer itineraries are available, featuring round-trip tours from Los Angeles or including the French Polynesian islands. Major cruise companies include **Princess** *(800-PRINCESS; www. princess.com)*; **Carnival** *(800-CARNIVAL; www.carnival.com)*; **Holland America** *(800-724-5425; www. hollandamerica.com)*; **Norwegian Cruise Line** *(800-327-7030; www. ncl.com)*; and **Royal Caribbean** *(866-562-7625; www.rccl.com)*.

GETTING AROUND

Island Hopping

Hawaiian Airlines *(800-367-5320; www.hawaiianairlines.com)* offers a daily service from western US gateway cities (San Francisco, Los Angeles, Oakland, San Jose, San Diego, Sacramento, Las Vegas, Phoenix, Portland and Seattle) and convenient and frequent interisland flights. **Island Air** *(800-323-3345; www.islandair.com)* offers interisland flights from Oahu and Maui. Daily ferry service is available from Oahu to Maui; ferries between Oahu, Kauai and the Big Island are scheduled to begin during 2009 *(check www.hawaiisu perferry.com/schedules/default.html for updates)*.

PRACTICAL INFORMATION

By Car

Of course, if you want to drive on the islands, you'll need to rent a car. **Alamo** (800-651-1223; www. alamo.com), **Avis** (800-321-3712; www.avis.com), **Budget** (800-526-6408; www.budget.com), **Dollar** (800-367-5171; www.dollar.com), **Hertz** (800-654-3011; www.hertz. com), **National** (800-227-7368; www.nationalcar.com) and **Thrifty** (800-847-4389; www.thrifty.com) all offer services on Oahu, Maui, the Big Island and Kauai. Dollar is the only national affiliate that operates on Lanai. You'll find Budget and Dollar on Molokai.

Honolulu is a big city with busy streets and traffic jams. On some of the other islands, you'll find plenty of narrow, twisty dirt roads, one-lane bridges and blind curves. On Lanai and Molokai, it's best to rent a four-wheel-drive vehicle to maneuver the muddy dirt roads that cover much of the island.

Driving in the US – Visitors bearing valid driver's licenses issued by their country of residence are not required to obtain an International Driver's License. Drivers must carry vehicle registration and/or rental contract, and proof of automobile insurance at all times. Gasoline is sold by the gallon (1 gal=3.78 liters). Vehicles in the US are driven on the right-hand side of the road.

By Public Transportation

On Oahu, **TheBus** (808-848-5555; www.thebus.org) operates a huge fleet of buses (including an increasing number of hybrid vehicles), covering the entire island and the airport. Look for well-marked stops and terminals near all major attractions and hotels in downtown Honolulu and Waikiki Beach, and in cities, neighborhoods and towns across the island. Fares are $2 for adults (one-way), $1 for children (ages 6–17). The Big Island's **Hele-On Bus** (808-961-8744) is free.

By Taxi

You'll find taxis lined up at the major airports; some are readily available at large hotels and resorts. Generally you must call a cab when you need one. Rates on the islands are currently about $3.10 for first 1/8-mile (1mile = 1.6km), 40¢ for each additional 1/8-mile, and 40¢ for each 45 seconds of waiting time.

Here's a list of Hawaii's major cab companies. Note: There is no taxi service on Lanai.

Oahu – TheCab (808-422-2222; www.thecabhawaii.com) and **Charley's Taxi** (808-531-1333; www.charleystaxi.com).

Maui – Maui Pleasant Taxi (808-276-9515) and **Islandwide Taxi** (808-874-8294).

Big Island – Laura's Taxi (808-326-5466) and **C&C Taxi** (808-329-6388).

Kauai – South Shore Taxi (808-742-1525; www.southshoretaxi. com) and **Kauai Taxi Company** (808-246-9554; www.lauhala.com/ kauaitaxi).

Molokai – Molokai Off-Road Tours and Taxi (808-553-3369; www.molokai.com/offroad).

ACCESSIBILITY

Disabled Travelers

Federal law requires that businesses provide access for the disabled, devices for the hearing impaired, and designated parking spaces. **For further information**, contact the Society for Accessible

Travel and Hospitality (SATH) *(212-447-7284; www.sath.org)*. All national parks have facilities for the disabled, and offer free or discounted passes; contact the National Park Service *(202-208-4747; www.nps.gov)*.

Passengers who will need assistance with train or bus travel should give advance notice to Amtrak *(800-872-7245 or 800-523-6590/TDD; www.amtrak.com)* or Greyhound *(800-752-4841 or 800-345-3109/TDD; www.greyhound.com)*. Book hand-controlled rental cars in advance with the rental company.

Local Lowdown – Contact the following agencies for detailed information about access for the disabled in Hawaii:
• The **Disability and Communication Access Board** publishes Hawaii Travelers Tips, including accessibility information at the five major airports *(available free; 808-586-8121; www.hawaii.gov/health/dcab)*.
• **Access Aloha Travel** specializes in providing travel services for disabled travelers in Hawaii *(808-545-1143 or 800-480-1143; www.accessalohatravel.com)*.
• On Oahu, **The Cab** *(808-422-2222; www.thecabhawaii.com)* and **The Bus** *(808-848-5555 or 808-852-6080/TTY; www.thebus.org)* provide public transportation services for the disabled.
The Hawaii County Mass Transit Agency *(808-961-8744)* provides wheelchair-accessible buses on the Big Island. **Maui Bus** *(808-270-7511)* offers wheelchair-accessible buses. **The County of Kauai Transportation Agency** *(808-241-6410)* offers accessible public transportation on Kauai.

• For beach wheelchairs and other equipment rentals on Oahu, contact **Hawaiian Islands Medical** *(808-597-8087; www.himed.cc)*. Contact **Gammie** *(888-540-4032; www.gammie.com)* for equipment rentals on Maui and Kauai. **Scootaround** *(888-441-7575; www.scootaround.com)* offers wheelchair and scooter rentals on the Big Island.

Many hotels, attractions and restaurants offer discounts to visitors aged 62 or older (proof of age may be required). The AARP (formerly the American Association of Retired Persons) offers discounts to its members *(601 E St. NW, Washington, DC 20049; 202-424-3410; www.aarp.*

ACCOMMODATIONS
For a list of suggested accommodations, see Hotels, pp177–189.

Hotel Reservation Services
RSVP Hawaii – 800-663-1118; www.rsvphawaii.com.
Accomodations Hawaii – 808-847-0761; www.accomodations-hawaii.com.
Maui Dream Vacations – 808-877-4816; www.mauidreamhawaii.com.
Hostels – A no-frills, inexpensive alternative to hotels, hostels are a great choice for budget travelers and students. Amenities vary, ranging from private oceanfront rooms and suites to dorm-style lodgings, on-site restaurants and guest kitchens, TV and Internet access, equipment rentals and tours. *For listings of hostels throughout Hawaii, visit www.hostelz.com or www.hostels.com.*

17

COMMUNICATIONS

Area Codes

To call between the islands, dial 1 + 808 + seven-digit number.
To dial between different area codes on the mainland, dial 1 + area code + seven-digit number. It's not necessary to use the area code to make a local call.
The area code for all the Hawaiian Islands is **808**.

Internet Access

Free wireless internet access is available across Chicago; see www.wififreespot.com/ha.html to find the nearest WiFi spot to you. There are also plenty of internet cafés in all the major cities on the islands.

Newspapers

Oahu's main daily newspapers are the morning *Honolulu Advertiser* and the afternoon *Honolulu Star-Bulletin*. Both papers feature extended entertainment sections, including a calendar of weekend events, in Friday's editions.
The alternative *Honolulu Weekly* offers a peek into local happenings. Other islands also have daily newspapers, including the *Hawaii Tribune-Herald* and *West Hawaii Today* on the Big Island; *Maui News* on Maui; and *The Garden Island* on Kauai.
You can pick up a copy *101 Things To Do*, which is published for Oahu, Maui, Kauai and the Big Island, at resorts and shopping centers. *This Week* magazine, featuring travel tips, activities and discount coupons for each of the major islands, is available free throughout the islands.

Learning the Lingo

Shaka (pinkie and thumb of the right hand is up, while the other fingers curl under, shaken side to side) is a greeting that can mean "way-to-go," "nice-to-see-you" or "be cool."

Aloha (ah-LOH-ha): Used for nearly everything good— hello, goodbye, love
Hale (ha-leh): House or building
Haole (how-leh): Foreigner
Kane (KAH-nay): Man
Keiki (kay-kee): Children
Mahalo (muh-HA-low): Thank you
Ohana (oh-HA-nah): Family
Ono (oh-noh): Delicious
Pupu (poo-poo): Appetizer
Wahine (wah-HE-nay): Woman

DISCOUNTS

Ther are two main discount cards to look out for:
Go Oahu – www.gooahucard.com
Go Maui – www.gomauicard.com
Both offer discounts on entry to major attractions, on a variety of tours, and also onmany activities.

ELECTRICITY

Voltage in the US is 120 volts AC/60 Hertz. Foreign-made appliances may need AC adapters (available at specialty travel and electronics stores) and North American flat-blade plugs.

MONEY AND CURRENCY EXCHANGE

Currency can be exchanged at most banks. Currency-exchange services are also available at Honolulu International Airport, but not at the other island airports. Some major stores on Oahu will accept Japanese Yen.

MUST KNOW

For cash transfers, **Western Union** *(800-325-6000; www.westernunion. com)* has agents throughout the Hawaiian Islands. Banks, stores, restaurants and hotels accept travelers' checks with picture identification. To report a lost or stolen credit card: **American Express®** *(800-528-4800)*; **Diners Club®** *(800-234-6377)*; **MasterCard®** *(800-307-7309)*; **Visa®** *(800-336-8472)*.

OPENING TIMES

Stores on all the Hawaiian Islands are generally open between 10am and 5pm, but many open earlier and some remain open until 9pm or later. It's best to try standard hours rather than risk the shops being closed.

SMOKING

Smoking is prohibited in enclosed or partially enclosed facilities, including airports, restaurants, clubs, within 20 feet of doorways, windows, and ventilation intakes, and in seating areas of sports arenas, stadiums and amphitheaters. Hotels may designate smoking rooms; if you wish to book one, specify this when making your reservation.

TAXES AND TIPPING

Prices displayed in Hawaii do not include the state sales tax of 4%, which is not reimbursable (1% sales-tax discount is given to citizens age 85 and older), or the hotel tax of 7.25%. It is customary to give a small gift of money—a tip—for services rendered, to waiters (15–20% of bill), porters ($1 per bag), hotel housekeeping staff ($1 per day) and cab drivers (15% of fare).

TIME ZONE

Sitting east of the International Date Line, the state of Hawaii has its own time zone: **Hawaiian Standard Time (HST)**. HST is two hours behind Pacific Standard Time (California) on the mainland, and five hours behind Eastern Standard Time (New York). Hawaii is ten hours behind Greenwich Mean Time.

Hawaii does not observe daylight-saving time. From the second Sunday in March to the first Sunday in November, add another hour to the time difference. Hawaii also falls an extra hour behind GMT during British Summer Time.

Getting Hitched in Hawaii

Hawaii's swaying palms, fragrant blooms and ocean vistas make the perfect backdrop for a wedding. You can download a marriage license application from www. hawaii.gov/doh.

For more information and ideas, go to:

- www.gohawaii.com/weddings
- www.bridaldreamhawaii.com
- www.alohaforeverhawaii
  weddings.com
- www.mauidforever.com
- www.ehow.com/how_
  172811_married-oahu.html.

The barefoot-with-leis beach front wedding has major appeal; other favorites are the **Byodo-In Temple**, a beautiful Buddhist temple on Oahu; botanical gardens with open-air chapels, even the Big Island's **Parker Ranch** *(see p41)*. On Maui, popular wedding venues include the summit of a volcano, a rain forest, or alongside a waterfall, where the mist creates a permanent rainbow.

HAWAIIAN ISLANDS

The islands of Hawaii are actually the tops of a huge mountain range that rises from the floor of the Pacific Ocean. Created ever so slowly by raging fires and spewing magma within a rift on the ocean floor, the islands grew layer by layer until they soared above the waves. Mother Nature sculpted the impossibly green landscape into dramatic peaks and valleys, encircled with a necklace of beaches in hues of black, white, red, green and gold. Glorious!

View over Waikiki Beach with Diamond Head in the background

Hawaii Tourism Authority/Joe Solem

Revealed in ancient chants, dances and stories passed on through the centuries, Hawaii's history is rich with tales of kings, queens and powerful gods ruling an isolated island paradise. Native Polynesians, who spread across the ocean and became Hawaiians over time, were attuned to the powers, and bounty, of the earth and the sea. When they sailed from the Marquesas and Tahiti—the first arrivals stepped ashore sometime after AD 400—they brought pigs, yams, taro, bananas and breadfruit. They called their new world 'aina (the land), as opposed to kai (the sea). When British captain James Cook, the first European to sight the islands, stepped ashore in 1778 with his crew, he renamed the archipelago the Sandwich Islands—after his sponsor, the Earl of Sandwich. After Cook was killed by Hawaiians in 1779 (see p46), no Western ships called in Hawaii for several years.

Getting Bigger All The Time

Surprisingly, this island chain is still growing. More than 80 volcanoes have bubbled from this Pacific hotspot over the last 44 million years. Since it began its present round of eruptions in 1983, Kilauea Volcano has added more than 500 new acres to the Big Island. Today, 20 miles off the coast of Hawaii, a new island is being born. Called **Loihi**, this infant islet is erupting in a red-hot flow beneath the sea.

The island of Hawaii was the home of King Kamehameha I (c. 1758–1819), who united the islands as he conquered other rival chiefs. Yet the monarchy lasted less than a century before pressure from Protestant missionaries, traders, whalers and sugar planters led to political change. Briefly a republic (1893–1898), Hawaii was annexed as a US territory in 1898 during the Spanish-American War.

In 1941 the Japanese bombing of Pearl Harbor propelled the US directly into World War II. When the war ended, tourism on Waikiki Beach exploded; later other islands, notably Maui and the Big Island, joined in the boom. With sugar and pineapple dominating its economy, Hawaii became the 50th US state in 1959.

Today each island seems to have its own vibe. For example, Oahu—home of Honolulu, the only large city in the state—has a cosmopolitan feel, while Kauai boasts a riot of blooms, with each garden more gorgeous than the last. Kauai is also the place many people envision when they think of Hawaii, thanks to movies like Jurassic Park, Blue Hawaii, and South Pacific. Maui is a funky place where artists and surfers merge in happy harmony, and the Big Island exhibits a rugged, rocky landscape that has a bit of an edge, thanks to its hissing volcanoes and roaring surf. Lanai, once the home of the world's largest pineapple plantation, draws luxury lovers to its posh hotels and manicured golf courses. Molokai is the antithesis of that. Set in the center of the island chain, it's pure Old Hawaii, not gussied up for tourists, a place where gorgeous beaches are nearly empty and one can still buy a burger for less than three bucks.

No matter which you choose, you'll feel far from the mainland US. Tossed like a lei into the blue Pacific, the Hawaiian islands are farther from any other landmass than any place else on earth. Their closest neighbors (though each is more than 2,000 miles away) are California and Tahiti. There's a dash of California's laid-back neo-hippie ambience here, and a touch of Tahiti's floral-scented exoticism, but there's also something uniquely Hawaiian about this place—worth seeking out and discovering.

The Fast Facts

- Seven of Hawaii's eight principal islands—with a total land area of 6,422 square miles—are inhabited.
- The largest and geologically youngest is the Island of Hawaii, more popularly known as "The Big Island."
- Kahoolawe is an uninhabited former bombing range; Niihau is a private island occupied by a couple of hundred native
- Oahu, home of Pearl Harbor and the state capital of Honolulu, is by far the most heavily populated island, home to more than 781,345 of the state's nearly 1.3 million people.
- The Hawaiian greeting *aloha* can mean hello, goodbye, love or welcome.

HAWAII, THE BIG ISLAND★★

The Big Island isn't your typical palmy paradise—its allure is big, bold and powerful. Hawaii is an island of contrasts, from the raw, primal beauty of **Hawaii Volcanoes National Park★★★** in the south to the glitzy resorts and manicured golf courses of the **Kohala Coast★**. Mother Nature is on grand display here, where the landscape showcases 11 out of 13 climate ecosystems, from subarctic mountain summits to eerie, lava-black deserts. To spend all your time here lazing on the beach would be missing the point—not that the beaches aren't wonderful, though. In fact, you could visit a different Big Island beach every day for a month and still not see them all. Even beach sand offers variety on this island; you can hop from black sand to gold to white to green. Visitor information: 808-961-5797 or 800-648-2441. www.bigisland.org.

Two volcanic mountains dominate the landscape. In the north, **Mauna Kea★★** (13,796 feet), long dormant, is home to several astronomical observatories. In the south, **Mauna Loa★** (13,677 feet) is considered active but is usually sleeping. Meanwhile, **Kilauea**, the world's most active volcano, has been a dramatic scene recently, with eruptions at Halemaumau crater on Kilauea's summit in 2008. On the north coast, the spectacular one-mile-wide **Waipio Valley★★** *(accessible only by foot or four-wheel-drive vehicle)* wedges

Fast Facts

The Big Island measures 4,028 square miles—nearly twice as large as all the rest of the Hawaiian Islands combined.

Because volcanic eruptions regularly add more lava to the shoreline, the Big Island is expanding.

For all its bulk, however, the Big Island is sparsely populated, with about 150,000 residents. In fact, cattle outnumber people here!

The island of Hawaii boasts 266 miles of coastline, not to mention the world's most active volcano, **Kilauea**.

Volcanic beach on the Big Island

Brigitta L. House/Michelin

Hilo★★

Move over, Seattle! Hilo, Hawaii, holds the record as America's wettest place, with 128 inches of wet stuff each year. Nobody seems to mind, since there's so much to do here. Tsunamis (aka tidal waves) are another story—this town has been ravaged twice (in 1946 and 1960) by towering walls of water. Many of the abandoned downtown buildings remain today, brightly painted Victorians dripping with funky charm; some are listed on the National Register of Historic Places. Lovers of exotic flora are in heaven here.

The Hilo area is home to Lili'uokalani Gardens, Hawaii Tropical Botanical Garden *(see p40)*, Nani Mau Gardens and more. The classic Hilo sight, though, is **Rainbow Falls★** *(see p34)*. Catch this 80-foot cascade in early morning or late afternoon, when the sun glints through the mango trees and creates prisms of color.

itself between 2,000-foot cliffs that funnel ribbon-like waterfalls onto a sandy ocean beach far below.

It's the adventurous traveler who discovers the Big Island's magic. Divers and snorkelers are drawn to the underwater world on the leeward side of Hawaii, where a watery landscape of caves, cliffs and tunnels reveals colorful tropical fish and other marine life. Kayakers explore the island's 266-mile coastline, where pristine coves and inlets await.

This is a place where you can hike (or ride horseback) in a crater, hunt for petroglyphs, hook a blue marlin, or catch sight of a rare bird or a migrating whale.

This is a place where you can ski and golf in the same day. And it's the only place on earth where you can drive up to a volcano *(see Kilauea, p30)*!

The Big Island has its historic side, too. The great monarch, **Kamehameha I** (1758–1819), was born on the Kohala Coast, and these shores were his base for conquest and unification.

Temples and ruins are tucked into the hillsides, often where you'd least expect them.

Volcano Viewing

Hawaii Volcanoes National Park recorded message: 808-985-6000. Kilauea eruption update: www.lavainfo.us.

The Hawaiian fire goddess, Pele, knows how to put on a show. In March 2008, Kilauea's summit experienced its first explosive eruption since 1924. The Kalapana viewing site on Highway 130 is a great vantage point for watching hot lava roll into the sea.

Brigitta L. House/Michelin

Waipio Valley

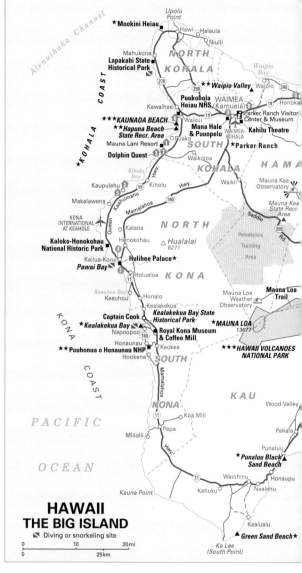

Upolu
Point

★ Mookini Heiau

Hawi – Halaula
Niulii

Alenuihaha Channel

Mahukona

NORTH
KOHALA

Lapakahi State
Historical Park

(270)

★★ Waipio Valley

Waipio
Bay

Waipio

(240)

Honoka

Puukohola
Heiau NHS

WAIMEA
(Kamuela)

(250)

Parker Ranch Visitor
Center & Museum

Kawaihae

Waikui

(19)

★★★ KAUNAOA BEACH

★★ Hapuna Beach
State Recr. Area

Puako

Mana Hale
& Puuopelu

SOUTH
KOHALA

Kahilu Theatre

WAIMEA-
KOHALA

★ Parker Ranch

Mauna Lani Resort

Dolphin Quest

Kiholo
Bay

Waikoloa

Waikii

HAMA

Kaupulehu

(19)

Kiholo

Hwy

Mauna Kea
Observatory

Kaahumanu

Makalawena

Mamalahoa

(190)

NORTH

Mauna Kea
State Recr.
Area

Saddle

(200)
Rd

KONA
INTERNATIONAL
AT KEAHOLE

Kalaoa

△ *Hualalai*
8271

Queen

Honokohau

Pohakuloa

Kaloko-Honokohau
National Historic Park

Training

Area

Kailua-Kona

Hulihee Palace ★

KONA

★ Pawai Bay

(1)

(11)

Holualoa

Keauhou Bay
Keauhou

Honalo

Mauna Loa
Weather
Observatory

Mauna Loa
Trail

Kealakekua

★ Captain Cook

*Kealakekua Bay State
Historical Park*

Mauna Loa
Weather
Observatory

★ Kealakekua Bay

Napoopoo

(160)

Royal Kona Museum
& Coffee Mill

Honaunau

★★ Puuhonua o Honaunau NHP

Keokea

★ MAUNA LOA
13677

Hookena

SOUTH

KAU

★★★ HAWAII VOLCANOES
NATIONAL PARK

KONA

COAST

Mamalahoa

Wood Valley

(11)

Koa Mill

Pahala

Papa

Miliolii

Hwy

Punaluu

★ Punaluu Black
Sand Beach

PACIFIC

Waiohinu

Honaupu

(11)

Kahuku

Naalehu

OCEAN

Kauna Point

Kaalualu

HAWAII
THE BIG ISLAND

🚩 Diving or snorkeling site

0	10	20mi

0	25km

Ka Lae
(South Point)

▲ Green Sand Beach ★

Hotels

- 🏠 Fairmont Orchid
- 🏠 Four Seasons Hualalai
- 🏠 Hilton Waikoloa Village
- 🏠 Kilauea Lodge
- 🏠 Kona Village Resort
- 🏠 Namakani Paio Cabins
- 🏠 Waikoloa Beach Mariott Resort
- 🏠 Waimea Gardens

Restaurants

- 🔴 Donatoni's 🏠
- ❶ Huggo's
- ❷ Ken's House of Pancakes
- 🔴 Kilauea Lodge Restaurant 🏠
- ❸ Merriman's
- ❹ Quinn's Almost by the Sea
- ❺ Tex's Drive In
- ❻ What's Shakin'

BEACHES

The Big Island is ringed with sandy stretches of gold, green and classic white, and they're all open to the public, even at the most exclusive resorts. Stretch out your towel and say relax.

Kaunaoa Beach (Mauna Kea Beach)★★★

Hwy. 19, behind the Mauna Kea Beach Hotel, Kohala Coast.

Despite the fact that beach authority Stephen P. Leatherman *(see box, right)*, once crowned it "America's Best Beach," Kaunaoa is still less crowded than nearby **Hapuna Beach**. All of Hawaii's beaches are public, so no worries about pulling out a beach blanket here. This quarter-mile crescent of white sand contrasts nicely with its lava headlands; beyond the beach rises a grassy slope and the manicured grounds of the Hapuna Beach Prince Hotel *(see p178).* Thanks to the hotel, the beach is clean and well-maintained. Rough water makes it a better beach for boogie-boarding and bodysurfing than swimming. Stick around to watch the sunset; this sultry spot is a wonderful destination for watch-ing the sun melt, sherbet-hued, into the water.

Dr. Beach

Director of the Laboratory for Coastal Research at Florida International University, Stephen P. Leatherman, aka "Dr. Beach," is America's most-quoted authority on beaches. In 1991 the Ph.D. in Coastal Sciences premiered his list of America's Best Beaches, which has become an annual event ever since. Leatherman's annual beachy accolades have become to tourism officials what the Oscars are to the movie industry. Some job!

Hapuna Beach State Recreation Area★★

Hwy. 19, 12mi north of Waikoloa. 808-974-6200. Open year-round daily, sunrise to sunset.

Hapuna, like most of the Big Island's white-sand beaches,

Hapuna Beach State Park

Hawaii's Big Island Visitor Bureau

is found on the Kohala Coast. (Look for black- and green-sand beaches on the south coast.) The best beach on the west coast (the dry side) of the island, Hapuna's half-mile stretch of sparkling sand leads to Cerulean water and the occasional lava-rock outcropping. Facilities include a picnic pavilion, a snack bar and a fairly icky set of restrooms. Bring your own beach toys; there are no vendors here.

Laupahoehoe Point Beach★★

Hwy. 19, Laupahoehoe, 25mi north of Hilo. Follow signs from Hwy. 19. Open year-round daily, sunrise to sunset.

As long as you don't expect a wide, sandy beach, you'll love this spot. A grassy area opens up to a wonderfully craggy stretch of lava-rock coastline, with pounding surf and dazzling ocean views. Camping is allowed here and the big picnic pavilion makes this a popular place with locals on Sunday afternoons. You'll get some wonderful photos on this beach and a pleasant dose of serenity, off

Touring Tip
The trailhead to Green Sand Beach is located at the base of Puuo Mahana cinder cone. Walk for 2.5 miles to the top of the cliff, and then climb down the cliff to the beach.
The unmarked trail begins at the rocky overhang here. Going over the edge of the cinder cone is the easiest way down; even this is a difficult and treacherous walk. Allow about an hour to reach the beach.

the tourist track. *Purchase camping permits ($6) directly from the Department of Parks and Recreation (25 Aupuni St., Hilo) or online (www.hawaii-county.com).*

Green Sand Beach★

3mi east of South Point (Ka Lae), Kau District. A 2.5mi drive by four-wheel-drive vehicle or an hour or so by foot. Check with your rental-car company to see if you're allowed to drive here; even with a four-wheel-drive, some companies forbid it.

You'll walk straight into the wind to get here, and once you do, the

Laupahoehoe Point

Hawaii's Big Island Visitor Bureau

Punaluu Black Sand Beach

Brigitta L. House/Michelin

surf is fierce and dangerous, but how often do you get a chance to see a green-sand beach? The olive-green-colored "sand" is actually made up of a mineral called olivine. Olivine is created when basaltic lava cools.

This semi-precious stone is also found in Iceland (the site of much geothermic activity) and on the moon. Nearby Ka Lae is the southernmost tip of the United States, and is also believed to be the first landfall of arriving Polynesians.

Punaluu Black Sand Beach★

Hwy. 11, 5mi west of Pahala.

Lava from the Kilauea Volcano obliterated the world-famous Kalapana Black Sand beach in the 1990s, but there are others to explore in Puna and Kau *(KAH-oo)*, near Hawaii Volcanoes National Park. Fringed with coconut palms, Punaluu offers the choicest setting for a swim in impossibly blue water. This picturesque stretch of shoreline is also a popular nesting spot for Hawaii's green sea turtles.

Green turtle on Punaluu Black Sand Beach

Brigitta L. House/Michelin

Color Me Sandy

Why do Hawaii's beaches come in so many colors? It's all about the raw material. White-sand beaches are composed of coral, pounded into a powder by powerful waves. Hawaii's black-sand beaches are, of course, made of lava rock—fairly coarse stuff that's hot to walk on and sticks like crazy to skin that's slathered with sticky sunblock.

The reddish-hued stuff at Red Sand Beach at Hana, on Maui, comes from the caldera of a cinder cone and is made up of finely ground red cinders. **Green Sand Beach★** *(see p27)* on the Big Island is a hidden gem with a gem-like color—an olive green, which contrasts nicely with azure sea and white surf !

PARKS AND NATURAL SITES

Hawaii's attractions include an active volcano (currently gushing steam and gas in a plume of white) and the most massive mountain on earth. (Climb it if you dare!) With all that, who needs a theme park?

Hawaii Volcanoes National Park★★★

Mamalahoa Hwy. (Hwy. 11), in Volcano, 28mi southwest of Hilo. 808-985-6000. www.nps.gov/havo. Open year-round daily. $10 per vehicle; pass good for 7 days.

This is the only National Park—not to mention one of the few places in the world—where casual travelers can visit a live volcano. At this 377-square-mile park, the major attraction is the wildly active Kilauea Volcano, and its simmering-but-sleepy neighbor, **Mauna Loa★**. The park encompasses the summit calderas of both of these, along with a rain forest, a desert, ancient petroglyphs, and the unique landscapes created by the force and drama of past eruptions. Unlike such deadly volcanoes as Mount St. Helens and Mount

Touring Tip
Most people drive through the park and feel they've done it all—indeed, you can see a lot by driving the park's Crater Rim Drive *(see p35)* and pulling off at key spots along the way. But the best way to really visit the park is to spend a couple of days hiking the weird lava landscapes or paths that snake through deserts, rain forests, and beaches (the park has 150 miles of trails).

You can camp in the park *(tent camping free; for details: 808-967-7321 or visit www.nps.gov/havo).*

Pinatubo, Hawaii's shield volcanoes produce slow, quiet eruptions, not violent explosions. Rather than fleeing Kilauea's spectacular fireworks, people show up and bring a picnic! The show is really something at night, when red-hot sparks splatter against a backdrop

Hawaii Tourism Japan

Offering to the volcano goddess Pele at the Halemaumau Crater.

Hawaii Tourism Authority/Kirk Lee Aeder

Lava from Kilauea Volcano meets the sea

of inky sky. Of course, lava flow has the potential to be dangerous; park rangers continually change hiking-trail routes as the lava changes its course. For eruption updates, visit volcano.wr.usgs.gov/kilaueastatus.php volcano.wr.usgs.gov/kilaueastatus.php

Park Highlights: Kilauea Visitor Center★★

On Crater Rim Dr., .25mi from the park entrance off Hwy. 11. Open year-round daily 7:45am–5pm. 808-985-6000.

Here you'll learn the secrets of volcanoes and how to view the craters safely. You can still stay at **Volcano House** *(808-967-7321; www.volcanohousehotel.com; see p53),* a rambling wooden hotel first built in 1846, which sits on the brink of Kilauea Volcano, at 4,000 feet elevation.

Kilauea Volcano★★★

Now is the perfect time to visit the Big Island. For the first time in nearly 25 years, Kilauea is extremely active. A major eruption in 2008 brought hordes of visitors to see what Pele, Hawaii's fire goddess, will be up to next. Currently, a plume of white steam and gas is gushing from the crater, flows of fiery lava are rolling from the down-slope of Kilauea into the sea

The Road Not Taken

The **Kau Desert** within Hawaii Volcanoes National Park is so similar to the moon's surface, NASA astronauts have trained for lunar landings here.

To get a peek at this eerie moonscape yourself, take the 9-mile Hilina Pali Road, off Chain of Craters Road at the 2.2-mile marker. Few tourists take this route, so you'll enjoy grand vistas of cliff, sea and sky in solitude when the road ends at the Hilina Pali Overlook. Remember, this isn't Disneyland: Whether you see a real show or visit during the volcano's "downtime" is up to Mother Nature—or, rather, the goddess Pele *(see p32)!*

For updates on volcanic activity, visit the Hawaiian Volcano Observatory website (www.hvo.wr.usgs.gov), or call the park's hotline (808-985-6000).

and occasional bursts of lava are exploding in remote spots on the upslope of the volcano, though it has calmed down a lot. (Conditions change constantly; check with the park for updates.) While parts of the park have been closed (mostly downwind of the crater where the eruption occurred due to elevated levels of sulfur dioxide in the air), there's great viewing in several places. These include the Jaggar overlook, along the wall by the Volcano House, and 25 miles down the coast, where the 2,000°F molten rock oozes into the water, creating a boiling sea and sending a plume of steam high into the sky.

Crater Rim Drive★★

The 11-mile Crater Rim Drive circles the great pit of **Halemaumau Crater★★**, which began erupting on March 11, 2008, with three gas explosions within the crater wall. Although the area around the viewing platform is currently closed due to sulfur dioxide fumes, this drive offers a look at the dramatic effects of volcanic activity, both past and present. Crater Rim Drive crosses the moonlike Kau Desert, where the **Thomas A. Jag-**

Touring Tip

Look for plumed Kalij pheasants, natives of Nepal that were brought to the island in 1962. Once you reach Mauna Loa Lookout, you'll appreciate the enormity of the mountain and, chances are, you'll feel very small! At the end of the road, the hiking trail begins.

---

gar Museum★ (see p47) displays geological exhibits and readings from inside the volcano. (**Note:** Crater Rim Drive is currently closed past the Jagger Museum due to volcanic activity.)

Mauna Loa★

Mauna Loa Road starts 2mi west of the entrance to Hawaii Volcanoes National Park, off Hwy. 11. The road climbs 3,000ft to the Mauna Loa Lookout, 13.5mi from Hwy. 11. Mauna Loa Trail begins where Mauna Loa Rd. ends, 14mi north of Hwy. 11. Call 808-965-6000 for maps and details.

At a mere 13,677 feet, Mauna Loa comes up short compared with Mauna Kea, the highest peak in

Plants growing on the lava shield by the Chain of Craters Road

Hawaii Tourism Japan

the Pacific. It is, however, the most massive mountain on earth, 100 times the size of Mount Rainier. Rising 18,000 feet from the floor of the Pacific Ocean, this perfectly shaped shield volcano is considered active, but last erupted in 1984. There are two ways to see it: by car or by foot.

Mauna Loa Road – The road climbs up 6,662 feet from Highway 11 to give you a good sense of the mountain. You'll drive through a curtain of rain forest to reach the **Mauna Loa Lookout**, taking a turn-off to see the lava trees. The phantom forest was created when lava flows engulfed trees and fossilized them. You'll also see Kipuka Puaulu, a forest grove that has escaped Mauna Loa's 37 eruptions unscathed. This is a quiet beauty of a spot, teeming with native plants, birds and insects, surrounded by fields of lava.

Mauna Loa Trail – This is 7.5 miles of perhaps the toughest hiking in Hawaii. It ascends from the Mauna Loa Lookout to a cabin at Red Hill, then 12 miles up to the Mauna Loa summit cabin at 13,250 feet. It's a 7,000-foot-high, steep route up, through a moonscape of lava flow. This is a serious trip, for those in excellent condition—only experienced hikers need apply! Expect to spend four days tackling the mountain, along with some advance planning (pre-registration is required). The climate is subarctic up here, with whiteouts and overnight temperatures below freezing year-round; snow in July is not uncommon. Altitude sickness is another issue and most hikers spend the night at the cabin at Red Hill to acclimatize themselves. Talk to the rangers at the park visitor center for more details. Hikers can also access Mauna Loa in by starting at the Mauna Loa Weather Observatory, via Saddle Road.

Mauna Kea★★

It's a one-hour drive from Hilo or Waimea to the Onizuka Center for International Astronomy (808-961-2180; www.ifa.hawaii.edu/info/vis; open daily 9am–10pm).
The drive to the summit takes 30–45 minutes. Take Saddle Rd. (Hwy. 200) from Hwy. 190, 19mi to Mauna Kea State Recreation Area. Go 9mi to the Summit Rd. turnoff at mile marker 28. A four-wheel-drive vehicle is necessary to get to Observatory Hill.

Pele
The goddess of fire and volcanoes, Pele, arrived in Hawaii by canoe, looking for a fiery dwelling place. As the legend goes, Pele moved south along the island chain, quickly fleeing the islands as her sister Namakaokahal, the goddess of the sea, attempted to destroy them. Ultimately, Pele found the perfect digs in the Halemaumau Crater of the Kilauea Volcano, where she resides to this day. Pele's love affairs and rivalries are the stuff of legend and literature here.
Locals say Pele appears to this day as a lovely woman dressed in red, or as a wizened crone who hitchhikes along the roadway. If you pass her by, you'll be cursed with car trouble. If you pick her up, she will vanish when you turn around to gaze at her.

Akaka Falls

Akaka Falls State Park★

Hwy. 220, 3.6mi southwest of Honomu. 808-974-6200. Open year-round daily (24 hours).

An easy-going, quarter-mile loop trail will get you to some of Hawaii's prettiest **waterfalls★**. Hike through a rain forest, along bamboo- and ginger-lined trails and past banks of wild orchids to get to the observation point of 442-foot Akaka Falls and its little sister, 100-foot Kahuna Falls.

Pua Ko Petroglyph Preserve★

On the northwest tip of the Big Island, off Hwy. 19.

Kamehameha the Great was born here on the Kohala Coast, which is as impressive as it gets in these parts! Add some of the oldest temples in Hawaii and a sprinkling of prehistoric petroglyphs, and you'll get a sense of why this region exudes such a special power. Admire more than 3,000 ancient rock paintings via a short hike just north of the **Fairmont Orchid** *(see p177)*; pick up a free map and brochure at the hotel.
The **Kona Village Resort** *(see p178)* boasts images that date back 900 years.

You'll feel as though you're at the top of the world here. Certainly, you're close—when measured from its base on the ocean floor, Mauna Kea reaches an amazing 32,000 feet (13,976 above sea level)! Set out into the Pacific, with clear skies and no light pollution, Mauna Kea is the best place on earth, they say, to stargaze *(see p48)*. No wonder that 11 nations have set up infrared telescopes here, to peer into space.
Prepare for a serious drive, in low gear. The 6-mile road climbs from 9,000 feet to nearly 14,000 feet. Once you arrive, you'll see the Keck Telescope—the world's largest—and 360-degree **views★★★** that defy description.
You'll also see Lake Waiau, a glacial lake that's one of the highest lakes in the world.

"Pineapple Powder": Skiing on Mauna Kea

Want to ski and swim on the same day? You can do it on the Big Island, if you're a hardcore skier! For four months of the year (Dec–Mar), the heights of Mauna Kea are covered with corn-textured snow. The volcano has no lifts, no ski shops, no grooming—but you won't wait in a lift line! If you're in good shape (altitude sickness applies at the lofty summit), the thrill of skiing on a volcano is a once-in-a-lifetime experience. *For details, contact Ski Guides Hawaii: 808-885-4188 or www.skihawaii.com.*

PARKS AND NATURAL SITES

Puako Petroglyphs Park

Hawaii's Big Island Visitor Bureau

These can be viewed from a boardwalk at the resort, designed like an old fishing village.

Touring Tip

At weekends, free summit tours depart from the visitor center at 1pm. Participants must be 17 and older, in good health, and have a four-wheel-drive vehicle. Stargazing is offered at the visitor center nightly *(6pm–10pm, free)* following an astronomy lecture. Dress warmly. Families are welcome.

Rainbow Falls★

*Waianuenue Ave., Hilo
(next to the hospital).
Open year-round daily 24 hours.*

Nestled amid a riot of colorful blooms, this waterfall tumbles 80 feet into a round natural pool. It gets its name from the play of early-morning sunshine on the waterspray, which creates thousands of tiny rainbows.

Rainbow Falls

Hawaii Tourism Authority/Kirk Lee Aeder

A Crash Course in Hawaiian-speak

Having trouble keeping Waimea straight from Wailoa and Waikoloa? It isn't you—there are only 12 letters in the Hawaiian alphabet (five vowels and seven consonants). The vowels are a, e, i, o, u; the consonants are h, k, l, m, n, p, and w. A quick tip for pronunciation: Most of the time, you must pronounce all of the vowels. Once you get the hang of it, melodious words like "Waianapanapa" and "Haleakala" will trip off your tongue naturally. It is rare to hear Hawaiian spoken in casual conversation, but the language is reflected in place names, street names, and in commonly-used words like "keiki" (children) and "mahalo" (thank you).

SCENIC DRIVES

See map pp 24–25. You've got to love a place where the scenery includes ancient lava fields, tumbling waterfalls, dense tangles of jungle, and Mother Nature's fireworks—an active volcano!

Touring Tip

Plan on one to three hours to cover Crater Rim Drive, depending on where and how long you stop. Start early in the day (**Kilauea Visitor Center★★** *opens at 7:45am*) if you plan to hike Devastation Trail, walk through the lava tube, and do the longer (but well worthwhile) 4-mile hike at **Kilauea Iki**. Add another 90 minutes to drive **Chain of Craters Road★★** *(a 38mi round-trip; see below)*, longer if you plan to hike the end of Chain of Craters Road. Wear hiking boots or other closed-toe shoes near lava.

Crater Rim Drive★★

Off Hwy. 11, in Hawaii Volcanoes National Park (28mi southwest of Hilo). $10 /vehicle; pass good for 7 days. For individual sight descriptions, see Parks and Natural Sites.

Yes, it will take the better part of a day to see everything along this 11-mile road, but how often do you get to peer into craters, walk on glossy black lava, and see the steaming vents of active volcanoes? Even if you don't have a whole day, at least do a drive-by, to take in the amazing lunarlike landscape of lava-rock hillsides plunging to the sea. (**Note:** portions of Crater Rim Dr. may be closed due to volcanic activity.)

Start at the Kilauea Visitor Center (on Crater Rim Dr., .25mi from the park entrance off Hwy. 11) and continue southwest on Crater Rim Drive.

You can see the steam vents from the car, but the small **Thomas A. Jaggar Museum★** *(3mi west of Volcano House; see p53)* is worth a stop to get a sense of the science of volcanology.

Next up: **Halemaumau Crater★★**, the site of the most recent eruption, and the most action over

Driving on the road cutting through the lava plain

Hawaii Tourism Japan

Thurston Lava Tube

Hawaii's Big Island Visitor Bureau

time *(typically, you can park and walk to the crater, but the viewing area is currently closed due to heavy content of sulfur dioxide in the air. Please check with the Kilauea Visitor Center, near the park entrance off Hwy. 11, for current conditions.)*
Along Crater Rim Road, you'll see blacker lava from a September 1982 eruption that looks like a torn-up road, with chunks of rock an inch thick. As you drive along, note the signs marking when lava flows occurred.

You'll want to pop out of the car to stroll the **Devastation Trail**, a half-mile path through a forest that was devastated by the eruption of Kilauea Iki in 1959.

This boardwalk trail looks fresher and greener than its name implies; back in 1959, lava, ash and hot gases roared into the sky from this tranquil spot, gushing some 1,900 feet into the air and turning the forest to cinders. Now, vegetation has sprouted up and softened the bleak landscape here.

If you continue along Crater Rim Drive, don't miss a stop at **Thurston Lava Tube★** *(2mi east of Volcano House; see p52).*
Across the street is the Kilauea Iki Crater Overlook, where you can peer into an enormous "frozen" lava lake, still steaming from the 1959 eruption. Want to get closer? There's a terrific **hike** that descends 400 feet through native rain forest into the crater, where you can wander across the lava lake. The park says it's a two-hour loop, but it can take a bit longer, so allow yourself plenty of daylight to do this.

Even if you don't go all the way down to the lake, it's worth hiking the beginning of this trail; it's a pretty rain-forest romp, with lovely views—a cool respite on a hot day.

Touring Tip

At Devastation Trail, you can connect with **Chain of Craters Road★★** *(see p37)* and follow it down to the lava flows, or continue along the loop of Crater Rim Drive.

Hiking Hawaii

Be flexible and be prepared. Those instructions are key when you're hiking in Hawaii. Weather and conditions can change abruptly—one minute, it's fine to swim in the pools along the waterfall; the next minute, rangers are advising people not to do it! Count on a sudden cloudburst, and bring a raincoat and a waterproof pack for your camera, even if it's sunny when you leave. Fog is common, especially in the rain forest. Pack snacks, and bring more water than you think you'll need. Stay on the trail, even if it's muddy; loose soil off-trail can send you sliding down a ravine. The forest service is good about closing trails if conditions are dangerous, so be flexible with your itinerary. There's always another lovely trail to explore!

Chain of Craters Road★★

Connects with Crater Rim Drive at Devastation Trail, Hawaii Volcanoes National Park. Allow at least 3 hours for the round-trip. For current lava conditions, call 808-985-6000 or check at the Kilauea Visitor Center.

This 38-mile road is one of the most spectacular drives in the world. The two-lane blacktop curves through a vast landscape of lava fields, descending 3,700 feet to the coast.

At times, the hillsides are rust-colored, where orangey lava and spiky vegetation slope toward the sea. In other places, fields of ropy pahoehoe lava are glossy and black, like chocolate syrup poured over a hot-fudge sundae.

Take a Hike – Park the car along the road, grab a bottle of water, put on a hat and sturdy shoes (lava can be cracked, uneven and slippery) and follow the path. Here, lava flows from several hundred years ago meet recent flows, and petrogyphs (images etched in lava) are numerous; look for the buried highway sign.

Lava flow is always changing, so you never know what you'll see. You might see flumes on the hillside, or steam clouds over the ocean, or, after dark, flowing lava and an eerie red glow in the distance.

Chain of Craters Road seen looking back from the hardened lava

Hawaii Tourism Japan

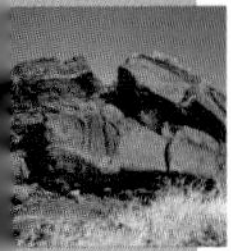

Pepeekeo Scenic Drive★

Off Hwy. 19, 4mi north of Hilo.

This little jog is worth a trip if you're heading from Hilo to Volcano Village or vice-versa. The 4-mile detour features wonderful views of lava-rock coastline, waterfalls and fragrant jungle.

Stop for a fruit smoothie at **What's Shakin'** *(27-999 Old Mamalahoa Hwy.; 808-964-3080; see p16)*, then follow the narrow road that winds alongside rain forest and ocean. Twisty vines fall like fringe from the roadsides, bridges are barely one lane—and traffic is two-way, so beware! Dense vegetation eventually falls away to a backdrop of sapphire blue. Stops along the way include **Hawaii Tropical Botanical Garden★★** *(27–717 Old Mamalahoa Hwy.; see p40)*, and, just beyond, the spectacular **Onomea Overlook**, where you can pull over to park and peek through a tangle of foliage for gorgeous views of too-blue-to-be-true Onomea Bay.

A short walk from the overlook leads to the **Onomea Foot Trail**, where you can walk along the shoreline and stretch your legs (they won't let you sneak into the botanical gardens, though).

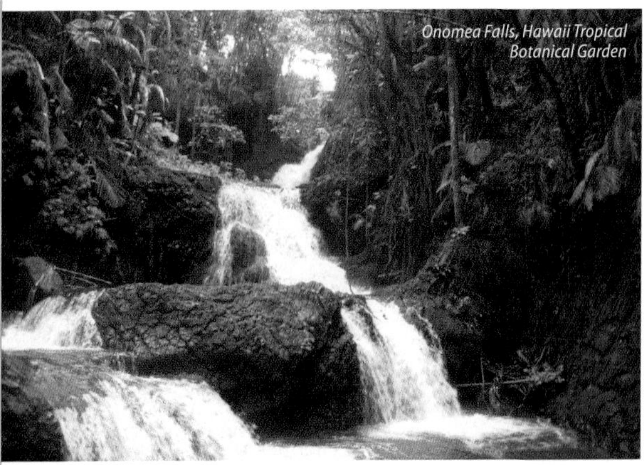

Touring Tip

Bring a picnic; there are tables at the base of the trail to Mauna Loa's summit.

Mauna Loa Road

Off Hwy. 11, 4mi west of Volcano Village.

At nearly 14,000 feet, Mauna Loa is not the highest—but is the biggest— mountain on earth. Its summit caldera is three-miles long; it last erupted in 1984.

While the trip to the top is a rigorous, four-day hike, the drive up (to 6,662 feet) provides a sense of the grandeur of this volcano. Stands of stately koa trees line the roadway, where, if you're lucky, you might catch a glimpse of the Kalij

Onomea Falls, Hawaii Tropical Botanical Garden

pheasant. One of the highlights is **Kipuka Puaulu**, or Bird Park, where an eruption 400 years ago resulted in pockets of untouched forest set within a sea of lava. A 1.2-mile loop meanders through this enchanted environment, where the air is full of birdsong.

Red Road

Hwy. 137, 27mi south of Hilo.

You'll feel like a local when you take a jaunt down this 14.6-mile-long old coastal road, originally paved with red lava. The stretch from Kalapana to Paradise Park features natural pools fed by volcanic springs, basalt cliffs, coconut groves, and black-sand beaches. A string of beach parks lines the shore; a local favorite is **Isaac Hale Park** at Pohoiki, where everyone goes on Sunday afternoons to fish, swim and picnic. Nearby, check out **Lava Tree State Monument**, off Highway 132, with its lava-wrapped koa trees *(808-974-6200; www.hawaii.gov; open year-round daily dawn–dusk)*.

Kohala Mountain Road

Hwy. 250, north of Waimea.

Most visitors miss this drive, but it's very scenic. Heading north from Waimea through the **Waipio Valley★★**, you'll reach **Upolu Point**, where a lookout offers great views of Maunas Loa and Kea, and Hualalai, plus the gorgeous Kohala coastline. The road ends in **Hawi**, home to a string of galleries and restaurants. Stretch your legs and then continue on to **Mookini Heiau★** *(temple closed due to the 2006 earthquake)* and **Kamehameha's Birthplace**. Follow the road to Pololu Valley, where you can follow a steep trail to a dazzling **black sand beach** (great for exploring but dangerous for swimming). Head back along stunning coastal Hwy 270.

Hawaii Tourism Authority/Kirk Lee Aeder

Black Sand Beach, West Kohala Coast

SCENIC DRIVES

39

GARDENS

Starkly beautiful though it may be, the island of Hawaii has lush pockets of tropical foliage, roadsides where wild impatiens and ginger grow in a riot of color, and a dazzling array of botanical gardens.

Hawaii Tropical Botanical Garden★★

Off Hwy. 19 on Pepeekeo Scenic Drive, Onomea Bay (8mi north of Hilo). 808-964-5233. www.htbg.com. Open year-round daily 9am–4pm. Closed Jan 1, Thanksgiving Day & Dec 25. $15.

Getting here is half the fun: The 4-mile **Pepeekeo Scenic Drive★** *(see p38)* is a rain-forest-lined twist of roadway, skirting cliffs that tumble to the sea.
You'll cross one-lane wooden bridges and get tantalizing glimpses of aqua waters as you follow the serpentine drive that leads, 1.5 miles in, to this tropical paradise set on Onomea Bay. *Onomea* means "good feeling," and you'll certainly pick up that vibe here. Set in a valley that slopes to the sea, this tamed jungle displays a variety of orchids, palms (some as tall as 100 feet), heliconias, gingers, bromeliads and other plants—more than 2,000 species at present, some rare and exotic. A three-tiered waterfall and natural streams add to the serenity of the setting.

Hawaii Tropical Botanical Garden

Brigitta L. House/Michelin

Touring Tip
Look for two-for-one admission coupons for many gardens and other island attractions in local tourist brochures like *101 Things to Do on the Big Island*, which is widely available in island visitor centers, hotels and many shops.

Wander through a torch-ginger forest, where some gingers stand sentry-like on 12-foot stalks, and meander through a banana grove. The golden bamboo grove positively thrums when breezes whistle through it. In addition to serving as a sanctuary for plants (including some endangered species), this garden serves as a living seed bank and study center for tropical trees and plants.
Tip: Can't get enough? Plan time for Amy Greenwell Ethnobotanical Gradens, run by Bishop Museum *(www.bishopmuseum.org)*.

Touring Tip
Mosquitoes thrive at Hawaii Tropical Botanical Garden, too. Happily, the garden staff provides bug repellent for visitors. Allow about two hours for a leisurely visit.

MUST SEE

HAWAII, THE BIG ISLAND

World Botanical Garden★★

Off Hwy. 19 near mile marker 16 in Umauma, Honomu. 808-963-5427. www.wbgi.com. Open year-round Mon–Sat 9am–5:30pm. Closed major holidays. $13.

Hawaii's largest botanical garden features some 5,000 species and other pleasant diversions, such as a children's hedge maze. Among the other nice touches here are free samples of juices from garden fruits in season, and a wheelchair-accessible rain-forest nature walk. The treat at the end of the bloom-edged trail is views of 300-foot Umauma Falls. Check out the Hawaii wellness garden, displaying medicinal endemic plants, and a garden planted with trees and plants arranged according to when they first appeared on earth.

Lili'uokalani Gardens

Banyan Dr., Hilo. 808-826-1053. Grounds open daily 24 hours.

Named after Hawaii's last queen, Lili'uokalani, this 30-acre park is the largest formal Japanese garden east of the Orient. Japonesque features include koi ponds, pagodas, and a moon bridge that makes an excellent photo opportunity. Cross the bridge to Coconut Island for views of Hilo Bay with a backdrop of mountains. The garden is located on Banyan Drive on the Waiakea Peninsula, where the towering trees have their own stories: many were planted in the 1930s by famous folk such as Babe Ruth and Amelia Earhart.

Pua Mau Place Botanical Gardens

10 Ala Kahua St., Kawaihae. 808-882-0888. www.puamau.org. Open year-round daily 9am–4pm. Donations requested.

This enchanting 45-acre desert garden rises over the ocean, with killer views of Maui (and sometimes whales, during winter months) across the Alenuihaha Channel. Fun features at this family-friendly spot include giant bronze insect sculptures, wandering peacocks, and a hibiscus maze with more than 200 varieties.

©Mila Zinkova/Wikimedia Commons

Heliconia, World Botanical Garden

HISTORIC SITES

From ancient idols and ruins to a lavish palace built of lava rock and coral, the island of Hawaii is an enchanting place to get an overview of the fascinating history of this island chain.

Great Wall, Puuhonua o Honaunau National Historical Park

Brigitta L. House/Michelin

Puuhonua o Honaunau National Historical Park★★

Hwy. 160, Honaunau, 22mi south of Kailua-Kona. 808-328-2288. www.nps.gov/puho. Open year-round daily, 7am–8pm. Visitor center open year-round daily 8am–5pm. Closed state holidays. $5 (pass good for 7 days).

During the 16C, defeated warriors and *kapu* (religious taboo) violators found refuge at this

Statues at Puuhonua o Honaunau National Historical Park

Brigitta L. House/Michelin

lava-black place by the sea. Places of refuge *(pu'uhonua)* were found on every island in ancient times. A lawbreaker who reached one of these sacred sites was purified by a priest; at that point, he could not be harmed by his pursuers, even after he left. Puuhonua o Honaunau is especially important because it holds the bones of 23 high chiefs.

Great Wall – An impressive, 1,000-foot-long rock wall marks the location of Puuhonua o Honaunau. Look for its reflection in the fishpond—this is also a wonderful place to frame a photo of a sherbet-hued Hawaiian sunset.

Self-guided Tour – Take a 30-minute walk around the 180-acre property and see the thatched huts, burial sites, temple, ancient idols and ruins, and canoes made in the old way—lashed together with coconut fiber. Along the way, you may see local canoe builders, wood carvers and other traditional craftspeople at work.

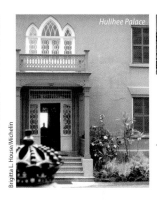

Hulihee Palace

Touring Tip

A great time to visit the historical park is the first weekend in July, when a cultural festival called **Establishment Day** is celebrated here, featuring crafts, music, hula and community net fishing. This is one of the best places on the island to get a sense of traditional Hawaiian ways. Bring a picnic and have lunch at one of the tables near the beach under a fringe of coconut palms. Later, walk the mile-long trail that leads along the coast past archeological sites where temples and homes once stood.

Hulihee Palace★

75-5719 Alii Dr., Kailua-Kona. 808-329-1877. www.huliheepalace.org. Visit by guided tour only, year-round Mon–Sat 9am–4pm; Sun 10am–4pm (last tour at 3pm). Closed major holidays. $6. (Limited tour schedule due to earthquake damage; call before you visit.)

Once the most elegant residence on the Big Island, Hulihee Palace was built in 1838 by the island's governor, John Adams Kuakini. Made of lava rock and coral mortar, the house served as the summer home of Hawaii's *ali'i* (royal family). You'll see beautiful koa furniture and 19C artifacts on the guided tour. The palace suffered major damage in the October 2006 earthquake, but it's structurally sound; fund-raising efforts are underway to finance $1 million for repairs. Try to plan your visit during one of their frequent concerts of Hawaiian music and hula, typically held at the palace the last Sunday of the month *(call for schedule)*.

Kona Historical Society's H.N. Greenwell Store

Mamalahoa Hwy., 14mi south of Kailua-Kona. 808-323-3222. www.konahistorical.org. Open Mon–Fri 10am–2pm. $7.

Constructed by Englishman Henry Nicholas Greenwell in 1875, and run by his wife Elizabeth, the oldest surviving store in Kona sold everything from salted salmon to saddle soap, poi to parasols.

Parker Ranch★

Kawaihae Rd. (Hwy. 19) & Mamalahoa Hwy. (Hwy. 190), Waimea-Kamuela. 808-885-7655. www.parkerranch.com. Houses open year-round Mon–Sat 10am–5pm. $9. Museum open year-round Mon–Sat 9am–5pm. Closed Jan 1, Thanksgiving Day & Dec 25. $7.

Experience the life of a Hawaiian paniolo (cowboy) at Parker Ranch. With about 150,000 acres and more than 35,000 head of cattle, these pasturelands make up one of the largest ranches in the US.

Horseback Rides

Get in touch with your inner paniolo on a horseback ride through the stone corrals and pasturelands of the Parker Ranch. Rides leave from the Blacksmith Shop on Pukalani Rd. and include stops at the rodeo arena and racetrack. Ages 7 and up; $79 per person.

Exhibits and a short film at the **Parker Ranch Visitor Center and John Palmer Parker Museum** *(Rte. 19, Waimea)* tell the history of the ranch, which began as a land grant from Kamehameha I to John Parker, a sailor from Massachusetts who married a Hawaiian princess and stayed to build his own cattle kingdom on Hawaii. **Mana Hale** – *On Hwy. 190, just outside Waimea-Kamuela. 808-885-5433. Visit by guided tour only Mon–Sat 9am–4pm. $9 (includes tour of Puuopelu).* The Parker family's original 1840s ranch house, whose name means "house of the spirit" in Hawaiian, once formed the centerpiece of the Parker lands. Today you can tour its handsome koa-wood interior, which includes handmade furnishings and Hawaiian quilts. **Puuopelu** – *On Hwy. 190, just outside Waimea/Kamuela. 808-885-5433. Visit by guided tour only Mon–Sat 9am–4pm. $9 (includes*

tour of Mana Hale). Named for the pretty knoll on which it sits, Puuopelu ("meeting place" in Hawaiian) now showcases former owner Richard Smart's fine collection of French Impressionist paintings and Chinese art.

Kaloko-Honokohau National Historic Park

Hwy. 19 (Queen Kaahumanu Hwy.), 3mi south of Kona International Airport, Keahole. 808-326-9057. www.nps.gov/kaho. Open year-round daily 8:30am–4pm. Closed state holidays.

Set at the base of the Hualalai Volcano on the Kona Coast, this 1,160-acre site marks an ancient Hawaiian settlement, stretching from mountain to sea. Wander past fishponds, *kahua* (house site platforms), *ki'i pohaku* (petroglyphs), *holua* (stone slides), and *heiau* (religious sites). On the

Parker Ranch

Brigitta L. House/Michelin

Aloha Festivals

This 50-plus-year-old traditional celebration is Hawaii's largest, featuring more than 300 events on six islands. Aloha Festivals *(800-852-7690; www.alohafestivals. com)* showcase Hawaii's traditions and history with special ceremonies, parades, carnivals, contests and arts and crafts, music and dance. More than a million people attend the two-month-long festival, which begins in September.

recreational side, there are hiking trails and good snorkeling in the crystalline waters of Honokohau Bay. Look for shore birds, sea turtles and, perhaps, an Hawaiian monk seal basking in the sun.

Lapakahi State Historical Park

Akoni Pule Hwy., N. Kohala. 808-882-6207. www.hawaiimu seums.org. Open year-round daily 8am–4pm. Closed state holidays.

From the 14C through the 19C, this site was a fishing village. Self-guided walking paths feature interpretive signs describing what it was like to fish the traditional way, with salt-making pans, nets, and fishing gear. You'll also stroll past thatched huts and fishing shrines, and visit an overlook where fishermen played a game similar to checkers while they waited for schools of fish to show up.

Touring Tip

They allow snorkeling just off the coral beach at Lapakahi State Historical Park.

Throw some clothes on over your swimsuit if you decide to come back and visit the site, though; they frown on visitors wearing bathing attire at the park facilities.

Lyman Museum & Mission House

276 Haili St., Hilo. 808-935-5021. www.lymanmuseum.org. Open year-round Mon–Sat 9:30am–4:30pm. Closed major holidays. $10/person, $21/family.

Mark Twain slept here. That's one of the claims to fame of the Lyman House, built in the 1830s by missionaries David and Sarah Lyman. Located in Hilo, the mission house is the oldest wooden structure on the Big Island, and one of the oldest in the state. The house served as a boarding school for young Hawaiian men, the Lyman family home, and as guest quarters for several notables, including Twain and many members of the Hawaiian ali'i (royal family). Exhibits feature furniture, tools and house-

Jill Maruyama/Lyman Museum
Lyman Museum and Mission House

HISTORIC SITES

hold items used by the Lymans and other missionary families, plus collections of seashells, minerals, ancient Chinese art, Hawaiian art and temporary exhibits.

Puukohola Heiau National Historic Site

2mi north of the intersection of Hwys. 19 & 270, Kawaihae. 808-882-7218. www.nps.gov/puhe. Open year-round daily 7:30am–4pm. Closed state holidays.

Ancient archeological sites mark the windswept coastline of north Kohala. Puukohola Heiau was built as a temple around 1550 and reconstructed in 1791 by Kamehameha I, who treacherously murdered his last Big Island rival here to dedicate the temple and make himself supreme chief. As British sailor John Young looked on, the king built the temple himself, along with his chiefs and commoners—men, women and children. A rival was sacrificed, so the war god Ku would be pleased. Hawaiian cultural and craft demonstrations are offered on Thursdays from January through

Captain Cook Monument, Kealakekua Bay

Hawaii Tourism Authority/Kirk Lee Aeder

September. Each August, the site hosts the Hawaiian Cultural Festival, with crafts, dance, traditional Hawaiian games and music.

• **Interpretive programs for children** are a highlight here; kids can take a hike, play ancient Hawaiian games, and become a Junior Ranger.
Tip: Looking for more great places to play outside on the island of Hawaii? Get to know these websites: www.hawaiistateporks.org and www.bigisland.org/parks.

Captain Cook

No name is more synonymous with exploration in the Pacific Ocean than that of Captain James Cook. He made three voyages between 1767 and 1779, and is credited with mapping the coasts of Australia and New Zealand, in addition to "discovering" numerous islands, including Tonga, New Caledonia, and Easter Island. Cook failed in his third voyage (1776–79) to find a northern passage from the Pacific to the Atlantic, though he traced the west coast of North America from Oregon to the Arctic Ocean.
When he arrived in Hawaii, the natives welcomed him warmly, perhaps mistaking him for the peripatetic god Lono. But Cook and several of his men were later killed by Hawaiians in a skirmish over a stolen boat at **Kealakekua Bay★**.
A town on the island's west coast bears his name.

MUSEUMS

The Island of Hawaii isn't exactly Museum Central, but the Jagger Museum is worth a peek (and a good spot to volcano-watch). If coffee is your addiction, the Kona tour will be your cup of tea... um, java.

Thomas A. Jaggar Museum★

At Hawaii Volcanoes National Park, on Hwy. 11 (28mi southwest of Hilo). 808-985-6000. Open year-round daily 8:30am–5pm. $10 (park entrance fee). See p31.

Amateur volcanologists can't resist this place, named for the professor who founded the Hawaiian Volcano Observatory next door *(closed to the public)*. Get awesome views of the **Halemaumau Crater★★**, a half-mile across and 1,000 feet deep; look west to see **Mauna Loa★★** in the distance. The museum is filled with seismometers and other fascinating stuff, so you can "see" every tiny earthquake on the island—there are several hundred tremors a day here! Videotapes show footage of days when the volcanoes spewed fountains of fire and ash into the sky, and spill red-hot rivers of lava down their slopes.

⚘Imloa Astronomy Center of Hawaii

600 Imloa Pl., Hilo. 808-969-9704. www.imloa hawaii.org. Open Tue–Sun 9am–4pm. $17.50 (includes one planetarium show).

They call it "an authentic voyage through time and space." Basically, this state-of-the-art facility—part of the University of Hawaii at Hilo, is a fabulous planetarium, with exhibits that explore connections between culture and astronomy. Text is presented in both English and Hawaiian.

Make Mine a Cuppa Kona

Kona coffee beans

What is it about Kona coffee? Grown only on a narrow, 20-mile-long strip of land on the mountain slopes above Kailua-Kona, Kona coffee is beloved by coffee connoisseurs all over the world. The first trees, a variety of Arabica from Ethiopa, were planted here more than 175 years ago. The combination of rich, volcanic soil and the region's distinctive weather worked like magic; now the Big Island is one of only two places in the US where coffee beans are grown commercially.

- About 4,000 beans are required to produce a pound of coffee.
- Each tree yields only enough coffee cherries (one bright-red coffee cherry contains two beans) to produce only about one pound of roasted beans each year.

FOR FUN

Big Fun on the Big island usually involves an outdoors pursuit... say, snorkeling with rays or stargazing on the summit of a volcano. And if golf is your passion, check out one of the island's 18 courses.

Stargaze on Mauna Kea★★

Got a sense of adventure, and a vehicle with four-wheel-drive? Drive to the 13,796-foot summit of Mauna Kea for some truly amazing stargazing. Dress in winter duds (it's chilly at the top!) and head up the narrow, winding, unpaved Saddle Road (Hwy. 200).

Check weather reports before you go, because Mauna Kea is off limits in bad weather—not to mention, you wouldn't see anything anyway. Make your first stop the visitor information station at Onizuka Center for International Astronomy, so you can get acclimatized to the thin air and altitude *(located partway up the mountain, at 9,300 foot elevation)*. As darkness falls, you'll stand in the midst of the largest collection of telescopes anywhere, at Mauna Kea Observatory. The stargazing here is unparalleled; the air above the mountain is exceptionally dry, cloud-free and

The Ironman Triathlon

Think you're buff and tough enough to compete with the best all-around athletes in the world? Each October, Kailua-Kona on the Big Island is home to the toughest multisport event around: the Ironman Triathlon World Championship. Nearly 1,700 elite athletes, from all 50 states and some 50 countries, compete in a 26-mile marathon, a 2.4-mile ocean swim, and a 112-mile bike ride. Spectators line up along the seawall on Alii Drive to see the 7am start. www.ironmanlive.com.

unpolluted. They say you can see 90 percent of all the stars visible from earth, right here.

Hawaii Forest & Trail – This offers 7- to 8-hour guided trips to the world's tallest volcano at sunset *(74-50358 Queen Kaahumanu Hwy., Kailua-Kona; 808-331-8505 or 800-464-1993; www.hawaii-forest.com; $185)*. Their naturalist-led trip

Gemini Telescope on the summit of Maunakea at sunrise

includes pick-up (from Waikoloa hotels), a picnic, and parkas—ages 16 and up.

Swim with Rays★

Rays can be found, most days, from as far north as Keahole Point down to Keauhou Bay. Most dive companies offer trips to dive and snorkel with the rays. For more information, call one of these Kona-based companies: Jack's Diving Locker (808-329-7585 or 800-345-4807; www.jacksdiving locker.com) or Hawaii Scuba Divers and Whale Watching Tours (808-324-4668 or 888-333-4668; konahonudivers.com).

The Big Island's Kona Coast is the perfect place to swim with the Darth Vader of the undersea world, the manta ray. Related to sharks, manta rays have no teeth and no tail stingers. (Note: this is not the kind of ray that killed Crocodile Hunter, Steve Irwin). They rely on their speed and aerodynamic design to outwit predators. The first thing you'll notice is, they're huge! The shy, typically harmless fish have triangular wings with spans that reach up to 20 feet across. Local divers have given these gentle giants names like Lefty and Nita Ray, distinguishing them by the patterns on their undersides. The best way to find rays is to join a diving trip (participants must be certified divers); dive-boat captains know where these intriguing fish are known to gather. They also arrange night dives to see the manta rays, one of the best things imaginable here. Divers must keep their distance, though, so these flying fish have plenty of room to maneuver. Manta rays are underwater acrobats, gliding, pivoting and somersaulting as they funnel plankton into their huge mouths. This trip is usually offered as a night dive, since the mantas and other sea life come to feed on plankton. (Plankton are attracted to dive lights). Mantas often follow divers back to the boat, and perform a farewell loop-de-loop!

Rundown on Rays:

- Manta rays *(Manta hamiltoni)* are the largest type of ray; they can weigh up to 3,000 pounds.
- In Hawaiian, rays are called hahalua; the name manta is Spanish for "cloak."

Manta ray

Hawaii Tourism Japan

FOR FUN

What a Way to Fly

Talk about a scenic overlook! For a great aerial aspect of the islands, and a look at places you otherwise wouldn't be able to see, a helicopter tour is your best bet. You'll peer into craters and see hidden valleys dripping with waterfalls. **Sunshine Helicopters** operates flights on Maui, Molokai, Kauai, and the Big Island *(for information, call 808-871-0722; www.sunshinehelicopters.com)*. **Tip:** A helicopter tour is an excellent way to get an overview of the erupting Haleakala volcano.

- Rays eat small fish, tiny shellfish and microscopic plankton. Since they feed on the bottom of the sea, a ray's mouth is located on the underside of its body.
- Females give birth to one to two babies at a time; each infant ray can weigh up to 25 pounds when it's born.
- Manta rays have been reported to jump 15 feet out of the water.

Watch for Whales

Captain Dan McSweeny's Whale Watch offers 3-hour tours departing from Honokohau Harbor in Kona, mid-Jul–May.
Whale sightings are guaranteed or you take another trip for free.
808-322-0028 or 888-942-5376; www.ilovewhales.com. $79.50.

Each year, from November to May, humpback whales cruise the warm waters of the Pacific to give birth and care for their young before swimming back home to Alaska. These gentle giants are so huge, you can see them from shore, but why not get a bit closer? Whale watch boats are crewed by marine scientists; some are equipped with a hydrophone so you can listen to whalesong underwater. Watch for a "spout"—the whale's exhalation—and the smaller "puff" that means a baby is nearby. Then, you may see a big black tail rise up and smack the surface of the water. If you're really lucky, you'll see a breach—the whale leaps out of the water and dives back in with a huge splash.

Humpback whale

©Dale Walsh/iStockphoto.com

Hike Kilauea Iki

Once you get a look at the sunken lava lake at the Kilauea Iki Crater Overlook at **Hawaii Volcanoes National Park★★★** *(Hwy. 11, in Volcano)*, you'll want to get closer. It's possible—and so worth it!—if you're willing to hike for about three hours.

The Hike – The 4-mile loop begins at the parking area for Kilauea Iki Crater Overlook *(across the street from Thurston Lava Tube, about 1.5mi from the Kilauea Visitor Center off Hwy. 11)*. Bring water and a windbreaker on this challenging hike; it's cool in the crater.

You'll start out with a breathtaking view of what's ahead, and then descend about 400 feet through dense rain forest.

The trail is pretty easy to follow, if somewhat steep at the beginning. As you get to the crater floor, look for ahu (rock piles) that mark the way. You'll pass the Puu Puai cinder cone and return along the crater's rim.

Hawai'i's Big Island Visitor Bureau

Kealakekua Bay

Pawai Bay

Here's another snorkeling fave on the west coast.

Set between Honokohau Harbor and Kailua Bay, Pawai Bay is accessible only by boat, and is a great spot to see dolphins, manta rays, and, if you're lucky, sea turtles. Boats that offer trips to Pawai Bay include **Honu Divers** *(808-324-4668; www.konahonudivers.com; $80)* and **Kamanu Charters** *(808-329-2021; www.kamanu.com; $80)*, who specialize in non-swimmers and first-time snorkelers. Both companies depart from the marina at Honokohau Harbor (2.5mi north of Kailua on Hwy. 19).

Snorkel at Kealakekua Bay State Historic Park

Some call this the best snorkel spot in the entire state. Located on the Big Island's west coast, this underwater marine preserve is a prime snorkeling destination. Schools of paintbox-hued tropical fish swirl amidst delicate fingers of pink and lavender coral and chunky pillow lava. Plus, the water is normally calm and clear, perfect for kids and first-timers. There are two ways to do it: on large catamarans and on small, rubber rafts. The former are great for families, since the powerboats offer onboard restrooms, food, a snorkeling lesson, and flotation rings.

- **Fair Wind Cruises** – Catamaran snorkel cruises depart from Keauhou *(808-322-2788; www.fair-wind.com; $75–$119)*.

- **Captain Zodiac Raft Expeditions** – Raft trips to **Kealakekua Bay★** depart from Honokohau Harbor *(2.5mi north of Kailua on Hwy. 19; 808-329-3199; www.captainzodiac.com; $90)*.

FOR KIDS

Kids who love adventure will be delighted by Thurston Lava Tube, a short but intriguing underground hike. Not your thing? See the cute (and free) Pana'ewa Rainforest Zoo & Gardens, just south of Hilo.

Thurston Lava Tube ★

At Hawaii Volcanoes National Park, on Hwy. 11. 808-985-6000. www.nps.gov/havo. Park open year-round daily 24 hours. $10/vehicle (park admission). See p36.

A theme-park ride, designed by Mother Nature! Hike through a fern-bedecked rain forest, with sound effects provided by native birds before reaching this giant hole-in-the-ground. The lava tube is dark with gnarly tree roots hanging down like bizarre chandeliers. Bring a flashlight and poke around.

PERFORMING ARTS

For a list of what's happening, visit www.gohawaii.com/arts. If you can swing it, plan your trip for the Merrie Monarch Hula Festival, the Big Kahuna of all the Big Island's events (week following Easter Sunday).

Kahilu Theater

67-1186 Lindsey Rd., Waimea-Kamuela (behind Parker Ranch Center). Box office: 808-885-6868. www.kahilutheater.org. Box office opens one hour prior to performances, whose times and ticket prices vary. Arrive one hour early for best seating.

Touring Tip

For pre-concert dining, try Merriman's restaurant, featuring innovative Hawaiian regional cuisine. As for post-concert dining, forget about it—this is paniolo (cowboy) country—cowboys go to bed early and wake up with the cows. None of that late-night stuff for them!

Kahilu Theater

Kahilu Theater/Bangarra

Hula, Hawaiian music groups and international stars take center stage here, at the "cultural heart" of the Big Island.

Recent acts have included the Lula Washington Dance Theater, Bela Fleck and the Flecktones, and the Lakota Sioux Dance Troupe—how's that for cultural variety?

HAWAII, THE BIG ISLAND

MUST DO

SHOPPING

There isn't much, but the choices are interesting. The better places to check out are Sig Zane, for stylish duds by a local designer, Big Island Candies, a local institution, and Waimea General Store (fun kitsch).

Hilo Farmers' Market

Kamehameha Ave. at Mamo St., Hilo. 808-933-1000. Open Wed & Sat, sunrise to 4pm. www.hilofarmersmarket.com.

Fish sausage, soursop, and puka-shell ankle bracelets—now that's one-stop shopping! More than 100 vendors set up shop here, offering fresh flowers, vibrant produce (including some exotic stuff you've never seen before), handicrafts and warm baked goods, "from dawn 'til it's gone," as they say.

Mountain Thunder Coffee Plantation

72–1027 Henry St., Kailua-Kona. 808-325-2136. www.mountainthunder.com

If you're a java junkie, the mere smell of this place will send you to heaven—and wait 'til you taste the organically grown Kona coffee!

Volcano Art Center Gallery
©Macario/Volcano Art Center

Located on the slopes of Hualalai, this family-owned plantation grows 100 acres of regular Kona and 45 acres grown organically. Check out daughter Brooke's homemade, all-natural line of body products, including the Kona Coffee Body Bar *($10)* and body scrub *($20)*.

Volcano Art Center Gallery

In Hawaii Volcanoes National Park, next to Kilauea Visitor Center. Mamalahoa Hwy. (Hwy. 11), Volcano (28mi southwest of Hilo). Open daily 9am–5pm. 808-967-8222. www.volcanoartcenter.org.

Does living near an active volcano inspire some primal creative spirit? Decide for yourself at the Volcano Art Center Gallery, where changing exhibits feature the works of nearly 300 artists, mostly from the Big Island. Paintings, woodcrafts, jewelry, mixed media, photography and more are represented, housed in the 1877 Volcano House, the original hotel in Hawaii Volcanoes National Park.

Volcano Art Center's **Niaulani Campus** is nestled in a native Hawaiian rain forest in Volcano Village. The non-profit arts and educational organization offers guided nature walks *(Mon 9:30am; 1hr; free)*, art lectures and demonstrations, readings, concerts, workshops, cultural and environmental programs, and much more.

NIGHTLIFE

Want to trade your flip-flops for some dancing shoes? Try Lulu's in Kailua-Kona (open-air deck, funky retro-surf decor, great pupus) and Uncle Mikey's in Hilo (hip hop, top 40s, Motley Crue cover bands).

Aha'aina Luau Banquet

At Kona Village Resort, Queen Kaahumanu Hwy., Kaupulehu. 808-325-5555. www.konavillage. com. Held Wed and Fri at 6pm.

Dance show at Kona Village Resort

Kona Village Resort

This is the longest-running luau on the Big Island, and arguably the best. The evening begins with a ceremony, when the pig is unearthed from an underground oven (chefs remove the hot stones that cover it with their bare hands as a sign of strength); then the feasting begins. It's a traditional Polynesian buffet that includes ahi poke, lomi salmon, taro chips, fresh limpets, coconut pudding and the kalua pig. The Polynesian revue that follows is an intriguing pastiche of South Pacific cultures, with *hula* (dance), *oli* (chants), *mele* (songs), the Samoan fire knife dance, and more.

Palace Theater

38 Haili St., Hilo. 808-934-7010. www.hilopalace.com.
This Neoclassical gem shows first-run movies and art films, and hosts concerts and theater performances.

Blue Dolphin

61-3616 Kawaihae Rd., Kawaihae. 808-882-7771.

This is the Big Island's best venue for live jazz. On Friday nights *(7pm–9:30pm)* local musicians jam with visiting jazz stars, and the result is always a heady mix. The Blue Dolphin is small, fun, and a pleasant change from the one-size-fits-all hotel bars around town.

Huggo's on the Rocks

75-5828 Kahakai Rd., next to Royal Kona Resort, Kailua-Kona. 808-329-1493. www.huggos.com.

Now this is a beach bar! Perched on the sandy edge of Kailua Bay, Huggo's is as close to the ocean as you can get without getting wet. Listen to the waves crash and order the Kiluaea, a concoction for two that arrives in a bowl spouting a pool of fire and sip—with caution—from two-foot-long straws. Live jazz and blues on Sunday and Wednesday nights.

HAWAII, THE BIG ISLAND

MUST DO

SPAS

Resort spas are definitely fabulous, but if they're not quite in your budget, here's a tip: Check out Mamalahoa Hot Tubs & Massage in upcountry Kealakekua, where the locals go for pampering.

Hualalai Sports Club and Spa

Four Seasons Resort Hualalai, 100 Kaaupulehu Dr., Kaaupulehu-Kona. 808-325-8000. www.fourseasons.com.

The only danger here is that you'll never want to leave! Fitness has never been so much fun, with choices ranging from a lava-rock snorkeling pond to an open-air gym. Water-related fitness activities are so numerous at this luxe resort, they offer guides (*alaka'i nalu*, or "leaders of the waves") to direct you. After your workout, report to the spa. Few can resist the body treatments here, each sounding more delicious than the last. Perhaps a Hualalai sugar scrub, with Hawaiian cane sugar, coconut, macadamia nut oil and honey, or maybe the Hualalai salt glo, with Hawaiian red clay?

Spa Without Walls

The Fairmont Orchid, 1 N. Kaniku Dr., Kohala. 808-885-2000. www.fairmont.com.

Fairmont Hotels and Resorts

Spa Without Walls, Fairmont Orchid

Imagine enjoying the long, rhythmic strokes of a lomilomi massage in an open-air cabana, surrounded by waterfalls, orchids and coconut palms. Fantasy becomes reality here, where massage *hale* (houses) are set along the waterfront, or nestled within tropical flora. Ahh!

Spa Terms—A Cheat Sheet

Here's a quick glossary of some you'll encounter in Hawaii:

Haipi – Haipi (Hawaiian for "pregnant") refers to a massage for expectant mothers.
Japanese furo bath – Uses gently bubbling water to relax and rejuvenate the body.
Lomilomi – A traditional Hawaiian massage technique employing a light, rolling motion. Lomilomi is said to restore the free flow of mana, or life force.
Noni/Nonu – This plant was used by ancient Polynesians to treat illnesses. Mineral-rich, it's now employed as a healing agent in facials and treatments.
Pohaku massage – Pohaku is Hawaiian for "stone." This is the local version of hot-stone therapy.

MAUI ★★

For more than a dozen years running, Maui has been voted one of the top islands in the world by a national travel magazine. Maui has great beaches, fab resorts and lively nightlife, so, who's to argue?
Visitor information: 808-244-3530 or www.visitmaui.com.

Maui no ka oi! This is the local motto, meaning "Maui is the best!" The T-shirts that read "Eat, Drink, and Be Maui," seem to sum up this island's attitude. There's a young, vibrant ambience here, where locals seem to feel outrageously blessed by their good fortune of living on Maui, and visitors tap into that feeling of goodwill. Of course, one has to make a living, even in paradise, and there's nothing low-key about tourism here. Local entrepreneurs have found a million and one ways to provide Island fun, from **ziplining** through the trees on the slopes of Haleakala (*see p70*), to tunneling through a lava tube in Hana (*see p68*). Not enough of a workout for you? How about a tour that combines kayaking, snorkeling and hiking? Well-heeled tourists find more than enough ways to spend their money on Maui, and also play a major role in

Fast Facts

- At 48 miles long and 26 miles wide, Maui is the second-largest island in the Hawaiian chain.
- Less than 20 percent of Maui is inhabited.
- Maui claims 120 miles of shoreline and 81 accessible beaches—that's more swimmable beaches than any of the other Hawaiian Islands.
- Maui is home to the world's largest dormant volcano, Haleakala. Hawaii's coldest temperature—11°F—was recorded on Haleakala's summit in 1961.

supporting the burgeoning arts community that draws inspiration from the island's glorious scenery. What attracts more than 2.5 million visitors to Maui each year? Certainly, the island's four marine preserves and spectacular coastline are strong draws, as is **Haleakala**, the island's mammoth

Lahaina Harbor

Hawaii Tourism Authority/ Tor Johnson

Haleakala National Park

Brigitta L. House/Michelin

volcano. Now dormant, Haleakala has left its mark on Maui's landscape. Haleakala ("House of the Sun") rises 10,023 feet, and boasts a moon-like crater surrounded by towering forests, waterfalls and jagged sea cliffs. What else would you expect but powerful beauty from an island named for the Polynesian demigod Maui, who managed to capture the sun as it rose from Haleakala's crater? Beautiful though it is, Maui is about more than good looks. Whether you're a surfer or a socialite, there's something about

the place that dictates simple pleasures—the sheer bliss of running barefoot on a beach, or admiring the countryside on horseback. Perhaps it's simply that Maui is blessed by the gods...

The Allure of Lahaina

There's nothing ordinary about the town of **Lahaina★★**, the hub of Maui's visitor scene: Lahaina is home to the biggest **banyan tree** in the US, shading almost an acre; it also boasts the biggest Buddha outside of Asia. Celebrated in James Michener's novel *Hawaii*, Lahaina exudes an atmosphere reminiscent of the 19C, when pious missionaries and rowdy whalers vied for the attentions—and affections—of native Hawaiians.

The whalers are long gone, but the whales remain an attraction. From November through June, the giant cetaceans play, mate and give birth offshore here before migrating to northern waters for the summer.

Other highlights: loads of outdoor expeditions, great eats... everything but parking. Since two million people visit Lahaina each year, and there seem to be about 15 parking spots, finding a parking space here may well be the most demanding activity on the island!

MAUI

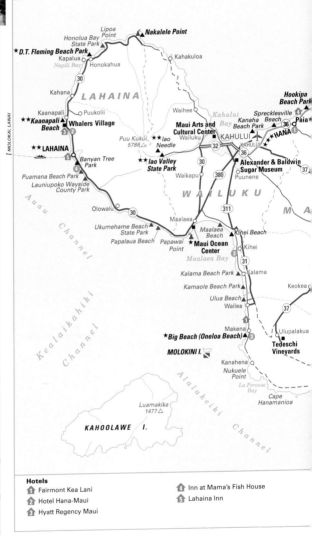

Hotels

1. Fairmont Kea Lani
2. Hotel Hana-Maui
3. Hyatt Regency Maui
4. Inn at Mama's Fish House
5. Lahaina Inn

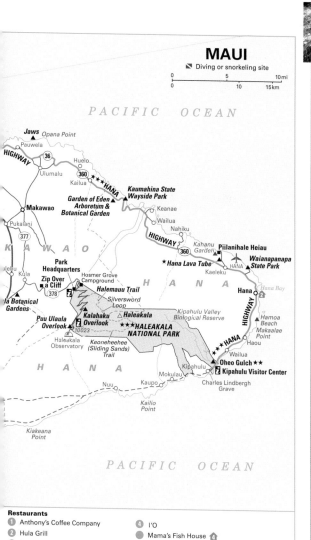

MAUI

◥ Diving or snorkeling site

```
0          5          10mi
0      5      10      15km
```

PACIFIC OCEAN

Jaws *Opana Point*
Pauwela
HIGHWAY 36
Huelo
Ulumalu
360 ★★★ HANA
Kailua
Kaumahina State
Wayside Park ▲
Garden of Eden
Arboretum &
Botanical Garden ▲
Keanae
Wailua
Nahiku
HIGHWAY
360
Kahanu
Garden
Piilanihale Heiau ▲
★ **Hana Lava Tube**
HANA
Kaeleku
Waianapanapa
State Park ▲
Makawao
KA   WA   O
Pukalani
Park
Headquarters
Hosmer Grove
Campground
Halemauu Trail
Silversword
Loop
Zip Over
a Cliff
378
Kula
HANA
377
Hana ░ *Hana Bay*
2
la Botanical
Gardens
Puu Ulaula
Overlook
△ **Haleakala**
10023
Kalahaku
Overlook
★★★ **HALEAKALA**
NATIONAL PARK
Kipahulu Valley
Biological Reserve
Hamoa
Beach
Makaalae
Point
Haou
Haleakala
Observatory
Keoneheehee
(Sliding Sands)
Trail
HANA
Mokulau
Kipahulu
★★★ HANA
Wailua
Oheo Gulch ★★
2 **Kipahulu Visitor Center**
Nuu
Kaupo
Charles Lindbergh
Grave
Kailio
Point
HANA
Kiakeana
Point

PACIFIC OCEAN

Restaurants

1 Anthony's Coffee Company
2 Hula Grill
3 Jawz Fish Tacos
4 I'O
● Mama's Fish House 🏠 4
● Nick's Fishmarket Maui 🏠

MAUI

59

BEACHES

Maui's beaches are always fabulous, but, arguably, they're best at sunset, when the sea turns to silver and the surfers appear in silhouette. This is one of those magical Maui moments—not to be missed!

Kaanapali Beach★★

Hwy. 30, 2mi north of Lahaina, in Kaanapali.

Kaanapali Beach

Hawaii Tourism Japan

Dubbed "Dig Me Beach," this is a see-and-be-seen place, where the tans are dark, the bikinis are tiny, and myriad beachside vendors are eager to take you parasailing or rent you a cabana. The three-mile-long beach backs up to a strand of resort hotels, as well as Whalers Village, home to waterfront restau-

rants and shopping. (**Tip**: Look for beach-only parking spots next to Whalers Village). A concrete path runs from Black Rock (a popular snorkeling area) to the Hyatt hotel. Kaanapali's tumbling surf makes it good for bodysurfing, too.
Stay late to catch the sunset. You might luck into an empty lounge chair where you can get cozy and watch night fall.

Big Beach★

Off Hwy. 31, Shoreline Rd., Makena.

Set in Southwest Maui, Big Beach (aka Oneloa Beach) is the largest undeveloped white-sand beach on the island. To find the beach, a good landmark is Jawz taco stand, across the street; to the right you'll find a parking lot. The surf can be rough, but the views are great. Locals set up tent villages here on Sunday and make a day of it. Had enough of that sticky swimsuit? Follow the beach west until you reach a path that climbs up lava rocks to Little Beach, where clothing-optional sunbathing is illegal but fairly common, nonetheless.

Wailea Beach★

Off Hwy. 31, just south of the Shops at Wailea, in Wailea.

A favorite of Stephen Leatherman *(aka Dr. Beach; see box, p26)*, Wailea is located in South Maui, behind the Grand Wailea and Four

Surfer Strip

During the winter months, waves deliver 4- to 20-foot faces at Hookipa, Honalua Bay and Hamoa Bay. Then there's **Jaws**, the huge, rideable waves located in Peahi Bay, east of Paia. These awesome waves rarely break, and faces can be big enough to fit a bus in, so Jaws is recommended for experts only. For a gentler ride, seek out Maui's south shores: Maalaea Harbor, Big Beach, and the string of beaches between Lahaina and Maalaea, including Papalaua, Ukumehame, and Launiupoko Wayside park.

MAUI

MUST SEE

Whale of a Time

Come November, more than 1,500 humpbacks arrive in the Hawaiian Islands to mate. They birth their two-ton babies in the warm waters, then head north again in April, to their Arctic feeding grounds. Large numbers of humpbacks congregate in the channel between Maui and Molokai. Maui has the largest whale-watching fleet in the islands *(for details, check online at www.visitmaui.com or contact the Pacific Whale Foundation, which sponsors cruises out of Lahaina Harbor, Dec–mid-May; 808-249-8811; www.mauie cocruises.com).*

Seasons hotels. Long and wide, this white-sand strip features high dunes, a sandy ocean bottom, and a shallow drop-off into deeper water. It's calm enough for snorkeling, a popular activity here.

🏄 Hookipa Beach Park

Hwy. 36, 6mi east of the intersection of Haleakala & Hana Hwys., about 2mi east of Paia.

North Maui's Hookipa Beach (*Hookipa* means "hospitality" in Hawaiian) is Windsurfer Central. Thanks to strong trade winds and consistent surf, Maui is Nirvana for board sailors, and Hookipa is the real deal. It's the most-photographed windsurfing site on the planet. Powerful rip currents, exposed reefs and snaggle-toothed lava rock make this one the perfect match for more experienced sailors. (If you're a newbie, get the hang of it at Kanaha Beach Park or Sprecklesville Beach first.)
There are several places on the island to rent equipment. If you'd rather just soak up the vibe, no worries. Windsurfers show up at 11am or so. The beach borders a coral reef, creating a shallow area that's great for kids. Beyond the reef, the northern swells churn up big, surfable waves.

Hamoa Beach

Haneo'o Rd, 2mi south of Hana.

Located just past the Hotel Hana-Mau, this salt-and-pepper beach is great for bodysurfing. Park along the road; stairs lead to the beach.

D.T. Fleming Beach Park★

Off Hwy. 30 on Napili Bay in west Maui, Kapalua

Named America's Best Beach in 2006 by Stephen Leatherman *(aka Dr. Beach; see box, p26),* this mile-long crescent of white sand is the unofficial beach of the Ritz-Carlton hotel.
Why should they have all the fun? Staffed with life guards, Fleming Beach is great for body- and boardsufing, and the tree-lined sea cliff is a perfect shady shelter for those who have had too much sun!

BEACHES

PARKS AND NATURAL SITES

Most visitors take in Maui's premier natural site, Haleakala Volcano, by car, at sunrise. Early morning traffic doesn't make for a peaceful escape. Instead, go at sunset, or hike the crater, or see it all by horseback.

Haleakala National Park★★★

36mi southeast of Kahului via Haleakala Hwy. (Rte. 37) to Rte. 377 to Rte. 378. 808-572-4400. www.nps.gov/hale. Park open year-round daily 24 hours. Visitor Center open year-round daily 8am–4pm. $10 per vehicle (pass is good for 3 days).

Tripping off the tongue as it does, the word *Haleakala (ha-lay-AH-ka-la)* means "house of the sun" in Hawaiian. According to myth, the god Maui climbed to the top of the Haleakala Volcano and lassoed the sun to force it to move more slowly across the Hawaiian sky. In turn, La, the sun god, agreed to slow his pace for half of the year so that people could enjoy longer days in summertime. Haleakala, now a dormant volcano, completely dominates the land-scape in east Maui. The spectacular desolation of its enormous crater valley—7.5 miles long, 2.5 miles wide and 3,000 feet deep—has been compared with the mountains of the moon.

Pastel hues of red, yellow and orange, as well as gray, purple, brown, black and pink, accent

Nene Bird

The endangered nene (pronounced nay-nay), also known as the Hawaiian goose, is Hawaii's state bird. Once hunted to near extinction, nene have been successfully bred in captivity and released back into the wild. You'll find wild nene populations in Maui's Haleakala National Park, in Hawaii Volcanoes National

Park and Mauna Loa on the Big Island; and along the Na Pali Coast on Kauai.

Hawaii Tourism Authority/Ron Dahlquist

Haleakala National Park

Brigitta L. Houge/Michelin

Stalking the Elusive Silversword

Also known as *ahinahina*, or gray-gray, silversword is among the rarest of plants. So rare is this relative of the common sunflower that it only grows at an elevation of 7,000 feet on the Haleakala Volcano on Maui. Another variety grows on the high slopes of Mauna Kea and Mauna Loa on the Big Island. Bursting from the ashy cinders of the volcano, the silversword erupts into bloom between June and October, sprouting a stalk from 3 to 9 feet tall. Pinecone shaped, the plant is covered with purple blossoms that emerge from the center of silvery, swordlike leaves. Look, but don't touch; these plants are a threatened species.

Brigitta L. House/Michelin

cliffsides and cinder cones. To truly experience the wonder of it, time your visit so you can watch the sunset from Haleakala's 1,023-foot summit. (Sunrise brings hordes of visitors, and traffic. Skip it.) Along the Haleakala Highway, the scenery changes from lush vegetation at the base to lurid lavascape at the top—over a span of 40 miles.

Park Highlights

Kalahaku Overlook – This is a good place to spy sprouts of silversword (*see box, above*). Silverswords bloom just one time per human generation, and then the plant promptly dies.

Puu Ulaula Overlook – Get to this overlook at sunset to take in the sweeping views. It's located near the visitor center.

Visitor Centers – You'll find maps and other information at the park's three visitor centers:

- **Park Headquarters** – *Near park entrance on Rte. 378. 808-572-4400. Open year-round daily 8am–4pm.*
- **Haleakala Visitor Center** – *11mi south of the park headquarters at Puu Ulaula summit. Open daily 6:30am–3:30pm.*
- **Kipahulu Visitor Center** – *10mi south of Hana on Hana Hwy., at the east end of the park. 808-248-7375. Open year-round daily 9am–5pm.*

Hiking and Camping in the Park

Thirty-six miles of trails crisscross the crater floor. Only experienced hikers should attempt these, and it takes twice as long to get out as it does to go in. The park service leads guided hikes daily, and an outfitter runs horseback rides to the floor of the caldera (*Pony Express Tours; 808-667-2200; www.ponyexpresstours.com*). If you're prepared for changeable conditions—rain, cold and wind—you're the type of camper who will enjoy sleeping near a volcano! **Hosmer Grove Campground** (*no permit required*) is located at 6,800 feet elevation, and connects with **Hosmer Grove Nature Loop**, a pretty, half-mile nature trail that meanders though a cloud forest. Campsites have grills, picnic tables, water and accessibility to toilets. The park also offers primitive campsites (*available by permit, issued at park headquarters*) and wilderness cabins.

Iao Valley State Park★★

Iao Valley Rd. (Hwy. 32), 5mi west of Wailuku. 808-587-0300. www.hawaiistateparks.org. Open year-round daily 7am–7pm.

Iao is the reason Maui was nick-named the "Valley Island." Ancient Hawaiians carried their royal dead into the valley for secret ceremonial burials. Now, the bright green cliffs and gurgling stream at the eroded core of an age-old volcano have made it a popular picnic and hiking venue. The 6.2-acre park is laced with hiking trails, including a short loop that crosses a stream and offers beautiful vistas of a velvet-green valley. The highlight here is **Iao Needle★★**, a basaltic spire that rises 1,200 feet above the 2,250-foot-high valley floor. A 1.5-mile trail meanders beneath cliffs that spout spectacular waterfalls after heavy rains.

Iao Stream with Iao Needle in background

Hawaii Tourism Authority/Ron Dahlquist

Oheo Gulch★★

On Pulaui Hwy., 10mi south of Hana. 808-248-7375. www.nps.gov/hale.

One of the highlights along the famed **Hana Highway★★★** *(see p65)* is Oheo Gulch, set in the Kipahulu District of **Haleakala National Park★★★** *(see p62).* At this picturesque spot, a series of small waterfalls tumbles from the southeast flank of Haleakala, feeding from one pool to another. These are often referred to as the Seven Sacred Pools—although there are two dozen of them, and the ancient Hawaiians apparently never regarded them as sacred!

• The simple marble grave of celebrated aviator **Charles Lindbergh** (1902–1974) rests on a promontory at the Palapala Hoomau Hawaiian Church, located 1.2 miles past Oheo Gulch.

Nakalele Point

Follow Hwy. 30 (Hana-Honoapii-lani Hwy.) 7mi north of Kapalua.

Set on Maui's western coast, Naka-lele Point is an otherworldly scene of twisted lava and hissing ocean. Standing out in stark contrast to its lush, green surroundings, the point is marked by a US Coast Guard lighthouse. Hike down the hill to the awesome blowhole below the beacon. The blowhole resulted when the sea wore away the shore below the lava shelf. Water now erupts from the hole like a geyser.

MUST SEE MAUI

SCENIC DRIVES

Local grocery stores sell T-shirts that read "I Survived the Road to Hana"! Drive it once, and you'll understand it. White knuckles aside, this is one of the prettiest drives in the world. *See map p 58–59.*

Hana Highway★★★

The road begins as Rte. 36 at Kahului Airport; it then becomes Rte. 360. 52mi.

Got nerves of steel? Then you can probably handle this hairy-but-lovely day-long journey. If you can't, there are tour companies that will be more than happy to handle the task, while you sit and ogle *(for information, contact the Maui Visitors Bureau; see p56).* Beyond-skinny curves and narrow bridges snake past rain-forested tangles of countryside that will make you feel as if you're driving through a botanical garden. You'll cruise at about 10mph around 500 curves, they say, flanked by great walls of bushy, Dr. Seuss-like trees in some spots, skinny bamboo and drippy waterfalls at others. The (barely) two-lane road is now in good condition after being first paved in 1984; it was truly a slice of

Touring Tip

Brigitta L. House/Michelin

They warn you to gas up and pack snacks before you attempt the Hana Highway, and the gas part is true. There are no gas stations past **Paia★** *(see p75)* until you reach Hana town. There are several fruit stands along the way; try some fresh coconut and homemade fruit smoothies. Start out early in the morning, as the highway tends to become more trafficked as the day goes on. Keep in mind that you must yield to oncoming traffic on the one-lane bridges. It's best to have two drivers on this exhausting route; you'll want to switch so each of you can enjoy the views. And finally, plan your trip so you're not driving the Hana Highway after dark.

Hawaii Tourism Japan

Large sugar cane farms on both sides of Hana Highway near Kahului Airport

Old Hawaii before it was modernized. Don't go too slowly, or you'll annoy the locals who use this as a commuting road. And be sure to honk your horn at the hairpin turns to warn oncoming traffic; whoever gets to the stop sign first has the right-of-way!

Along the Hana Highway

Garden of Eden Botanical Gardens and Arboretum – *Mile marker 10 1/2. 808-572-9899. www. mauigardenofeden.com. Open year-round daily 8am–3pm. $10.*
If this garden looks familiar, it's because scenes from *Jurassic Park* were filmed here. Walk the trails, have a picnic, and enjoy views of jungly hillsides and rocky coast.
Kaumahina State Wayside Park – *Mile marker 12.* Alas, the access to Puohokamoa Falls has been closed due to accidents, but you'll want to get out and stretch your legs here, where gardens burst with torch and shell gingers. An unmarked trail meanders through a eucalyptus forest. Admire sweeping views of the ocean, just a short walk to the left of the parking lot.
Waianapanapa State Park – *Mile marker 32. 808-248-4843. Open year-round daily dawn–dusk.* Considered one of the must-stops on the Hana Highway, this park gets busy, but it's worth a visit. **Attractions** include a black-sand beach, caves, and cave pools for swimming. Take a short hike along an ancient lava rock footpath for dramatic views of sea caves and the shoreline.
Hana – *At the end of Rte. 360.* Hana (population 1,856) is home to the inviting **Hotel Hana-Maui**, *(see p180)*, the Hana Coast Gallery, the Hasegawa General Store and a gas station. Stop at the general store for items you didn't know you needed, like flip-flop socks and Spam sushi. Just south of town, follow the signs to Hamoa Beach, a swath of sand that James Michener compared favorably with the beaches of the South Pacific. A hike up to Fagan Memorial Cross reveals the best views of Hana town and the coastline.

Road to Hana

Hawaii Tourism Authority/ Tor Johnson

MUSEUMS

Talk about raising cane. At one time, there were 80 sugar plantations in Hawaii; now there are two. (One is next door to the museum.)

Alexander & Baldwin Sugar Museum

Puunene Ave & Hansen Rd., Puunene. 808-871-8058. www.sug armuseum.com. Open year-round Mon–Sat 9:30am–4:30pm. Closed major holidays. $7.

Smelling pleasantly of molasses, this museum chronicles the interplay of geography, water and people in growing sugarcane and producing sugar. Immigrant workers arrived in the mid-19C; their presence helped make Hawaii the melting pot it is today.

GARDENS

This picture-pretty spot in upcountry Maui features native plants, an aviary, with nene geese, and great views of western mountains.

☘ Kula Botanical Garden

Hwy. 377 (Kekaulike Ave.), 1mi from junction of Hwys. 377 & 37. 808-878-1715. www.kulabotani calgarden.com. Open year-round Mon–Sat 9am–4pm. Closed major holidays. $7.50.

For a sense of what Hawaii might have looked like before the

Polynesians arrived on the islands (bringing their own plants and animals by canoe), take a look at the collection of native plants here. This eight-acre site, perched at an elevation of 3,300 feet, features orchids, proteas, bromeliads, poisonous plants, native fauna, even the mighty koa tree, a broadleaf evergreen that can reach heights of 100 feet.

HISTORIC SITES

The largest ancient temple ruins in Hawaii, Piilanihale is set within Kahunu Garden, a 294-acre plot lush with breadfruit trees and bamboo.

Piilanihale Heiau

On Hana Hwy., at the Kahanu Garden. 808-248-8912. www.ntbg. org. Open year-round daily 10am–2pm. Closed major holidays. Access will be closed if river is too high (flash flood area). $10.

Overlooking the Hana coastline, just north of town, Piilanihale is the largest temple in Hawaii, with walls rising to 90 feet high. The temple was built by King Piilani during the late 14C, and is still maintained by his descendents. So powerful is the temple's energy force that pilots approaching Hana Airport refuse to fly over it

FOR FUN

Nothing says 'fun' like wriggling through a lava tube—unless it's biking down a volcano! Looking for a more mellow pursuit? Sample some pineapple or passionfruit wine.

Hana Lava Tube★

205 Ulaino Rd., Hana (turn onto Ulaino Rd. at mile marker 31, and drive .4mi to cave). 808-248-7308; www.mauicave. com. Self-guided tours Mon–Sat, 10:30am–3:30pm. $12.

Don a hard hat and a flashlight and head into one of the world's largest volcanic lava tubes. No tight passages here (except the optional tiny chamber), so it's an easy walk into an underground lavascape of stalactites, stalagmites, and flowstone. The flowstone looks like chocolate syrup in some spots, candy kisses in others. Interpretive signage describes how the cavern was formed. They also offer wild cave tours for adventurous types. Also on the grounds is the Red Ti Botanical Maze, worth a peek if you're not in a hurry.

🚴 Bike Down a Volcano

Several companies rent mountain bikes and offer guided bike tours to Haleakala. Some companies specify a height or minimum age requirement (call to check before you go—see p69 for outfitters to contact). Rental prices start at about $35 per day; tour prices are about $125 and up. (Look for online discounts.)

Imagine biking down the slopes of a volcano with a backdrop of fiery sunrise. Biking down Haleakala ("House of the Sun" in Hawaiian) is a true Maui adventure. While the park service has currently suspended bike tours from the volcano's 10,000-foot summit, you can still join a tour group and begin your ride at 6,500 feet. Choose a tour that goes from Haleakala to the beach town of Paia (28 miles) or to an upcountry

Biking down Haleakala

©Sheldon Kralstein/iStockphoto.com

MAUI

MUST DO

Free Hula for You-la

You might luck into a free Hawaiian dance performance in Lahaina's **Banyan Tree Park** (*off Front St. in downtown Lahaina*) if you visit during one of the many annual festivals (*see pp10–11*).

You'll discover that hula isn't the hip-shaking extravaganza as depicted by Hollywood in *Blue Hawaii*; it's a serious art form. Hula Kahiko (traditional) is performed mainly with percussion instruments, while Hula Auana (contemporary) typically features ukuleles, acoustic and steel guitars and bass.

Hawaii Tourism Authority/Kirk Lee Aeder

winery (20 miles). Not a bad way to spend a morning! Guided tours will take you up the volcano by van, provide gear, and ride with you as you glide down the mountain.

Rather do it yourself? Your outfitter will rent you gear and transport you to the park. Rent for the day or the week; they'll also supply maps and advice on good routes. Average speed is 15–20mph, slowing down for turns and curves. Expect some wild belly-flips as you career down the mountain!

The following **outfitters** will get you rolling:

- **Haleakala Bike Company** – *888-922-2453. www.bikemaui.com.*
- **Maui Sunriders** – *866-500-2453. www.mauibikeride.com.*
- **Maui Mountain Cruisers** – *808-871-6014 or 800-232-6284. www.mauimountaincruisers.com.*
- **Maui Downhill Volcano Rides** – *808-871-2155 or 800-535-2453. www.mauidownhill.com.*

Tedeschi Vineyards

Tedeschi Vineyards, Rte. 37 (Haleakala Hwy.), Ulupalakua. 808-878-6058. www.mauiwine. com. Free tours daily, 10:30am & 1:30pm.

Located in upcountry Maui, on the slopes of Haleakala, these vineyards sit on Ulupalakua Ranch, where cowboys still herd cattle. The pasturelands are beautiful, as are the views of the golden-sand-laced Kihei coastline below. Stroll the grounds, and sample some of the wines they make from grapes, pineapples and raspberries.

The tasting room is housed in a renovated cottage; note the cool bar, cut from the trunk of a mango tree. Maui Blanc, made from pineapples, is a pleasant, and popular,

Tedeschi Vineyards

Hawaii Tourism Europe

FOR FUN

wine. Maui Blush is sweetened by passionfruit. Most wines cost about $12 per bottle and up.

Pipiwai Trail

Follow the Hana Hwy. south to Haleakala National Park entrance at Kipahulu (10mi south of Hana). $10 park admission. Trail is located across the street from parking lot.

This 3.7-mile trail offers rewards aplenty, including a sweet-smelling guava forest, an eerily dark bamboo grove, and two sets of waterfalls, including 400-foot Waikomo Falls. Plan on three hours, so you can meander.

Zip Over a Cliff

Skyline Eco-Adventures, Hwy. 378 (Crater Rd.), Kula; 808-878-8400; www.skylinehawaii.com. $89. Also offered in Kaanapali (eight ziplines); trip meets at the Fairway Shops. $150 (includes lunch).

Ziplining is catching on everywhere, and Maui is no exception. After a pretty, half-mile hike through a forest, you'll walk to the edge of the valley, get strapped into a harness, and soar over gulches, cliffs and valleys on a zipline strung on the slopes of Haleakala. You can do this five times if you choose—they have five ziplines strung through this property on Haleakala Ranch. They've been doing this since 2002—so far, so good! And, they promise, once you've done it, you're thoroughly hooked (or perhaps they're just stringing us along!) And if you get into the harness and decide, "Nah!", no worries! (This is Maui, after all!)

Learn to Surf

Maui Waveriders meets at two locations: 133 Prison St. in Lahaina and 1975 S. Kihei Rd. in Kihei. 808-875-4761; www.mauiwaveriders. com. Two-hour group lessons, $60 adults, $50, kids age 7 and up. Private lessons, $130. Private lessons are available for kids under age 7.

"If you don't have fun, and you don't ride a wave, you don't pay," according to the Castleton family, who run Maui Waveriders—and so far, they say, only one person has asked for a refund! They say they can teach you to surf in one easy

More Great Hikes on Maui

Sliding Sands Trail

Halemauu Trail to **Valley Rim** is an easy two-mile-plus walk featuring spectacular views of the Hana coastline *(in Haleakala National Park; trailhead is located on the road to Puu Ulaula Overlook).* If you're in good shape, try the strenuous **Keoneheehee Trail**, also called **Sliding Sands Trail** *(also in the park; trailhead is located near the Visitor Center parking lot).* It's a difficult half-day hike to the first cinder cone—an elevation change of 2,800 feet in 4 miles—but it's a once-in-a-lifetime experience of the breathtaking Mars-like landscape of red, orange, silver and blue cinder cones within the crater.

Molokini Island

lesson—cowards and non-swimmers included. Classes are organized by age group and families; after the two-hour lesson, surfer wannabes can give it a go on their own if boards are available. Along with form and technique, you'll learn water safety and surfing etiquette—you'll be a surfer dude or surfer chick in no time!

As far as **surfing on Maui** goes, the south shore boasts some gentle breaks that are great for beginners, including the "fastest right in the world" at 🏄 **Maalaea Harbor**, north of Kihei on the west coast. Honolua Bay, on the northwest tip of the island, is famous for its winter waves, which can range in size from 4- to 20-foot faces! Then there's **Jaws** *(see p60)*, the mother of all waves, in Peahi Bay, where the enormous swells are truly jaw-dropping and for experts only.

Snorkel off Molokini Island★★

Excursions cited below depart from Maalaea Harbor, off Hwy. 30. Prices start at $80 and up; check websites for online discounts.

Three miles off Makena on Maui's west coast lies an enchanting crescent of Crater Rim known as Molokini Island. Eighteen-acre Molokini rises 160 feet above waters filled with coral heads and a dazzling array of tropical fishes. This protected area, a Marine Conservation District, is irresistible to snorkelers and divers. Molokini is also a seabird sanctuary, and a great place to see migrating whales in season (Dec–May). Don't miss it!

Boats run year-round from Maalaea and Lahaina. Companies who run trips to the island include **Trilogy Excursions** *(808-674-5649; www.sailtrilogy.com)*, **Pride of Maui** *(877-867-7433; www.prideof maui.com)*, and **Maui Classic Charters** *(800-736-5740; www.mauiclassiccharters.com)*.

Windsurfing on Maui

People move to Maui just for the windsurfing—that's how awesome it is! Expert board sailors go airborne at **Hookipa Beach Park**, taking advantage of the strong trade winds that blow in from the north *(Hwy. 36, 6mi east*

FOR FUN

of the intersection of Haleakala & Hana Hwys.; see p61). Everyone else heads to the gentler waters at **Spreckelsville** and **Kanaha** (west of Hookipa Beach on the north coast), as well as Kihei Beach (on the west coast at the junction of Hwys. 311 & 31) for lessons and practice. No need to plan ahead for lessons; windsurfing schools often set up shop on the beach. You can rent gear at one of the many sports shops in Paia, Wailuku and Kahului.

Snorkel trip to Lanai★

Meet at slip 16, Lahaina Harbor. 808-661-7670. www.safariboat excursions.com. Trips offered mid-Apr through Dec. No children under age 5.

Everybody raves about Captain Dave's "safaris" to Lanai. And why not? You'll see pristine spots most tourists never encounter, and snorkel amidst lava formations and hidden caves. Trips last a half-day and include lunch (good veggie options, too).

Whale Watching

Few things are more thrilling to kids—and adults—than seeing a whale in the wild. Whale season in Hawaii runs roughly from December through April, before the massive cetaceans head north to their Arctic feeding grounds.

Windsurfing in Maui

Hawaii Tourism Authority/Ron Dahlquist

Respect for the whales is a big deal here; during whale season, personal watercraft and parasail boats are prohibited.

There's no lack of whale-watching excursions in Maui, but the most well-regarded of these is operated by the Pacific Whale Foundation (808-249-5311 or 800-942-5311; www.mauiecocruises.com). This nonprofit group, a marine research and conservation organization, runs trips led by certified natural-ists. They report a 99 percent suc-cess rate seeing whales; trips run from December to mid-May. Cool feature: You can listen to whale song on underwater hydrophones. Trips depart from Lahaina and Maalaea Harbor ($28.75–$31.95 adults, $15.30–$17 children ages 7–12, free for ages 6 and under). Look for discount coupons on their website.

See? Turtles.

If you're lucky enough, you'll go flipper-to-flipper with a **honu** while you're snorkeling or diving in Hawaii. A honu is a green sea turtle (Chelonia mydas), an endangered species that feeds in coastal waters around the Hawaiian Islands. Adults can weigh up to 400 pounds, with a carapace (upper shell) around 3.5 feet long. Why are green sea turtles green? They feed mainly on algae.

FOR KIDS

Teens and older kids thrill to Maui's wild outdoors scene, with opportunities to surf, windsurf and snorkel at every turn.
For little ones, nothing beats the chance to see wild creatures (from a safe distance!)

Maui Ocean Center ★

192 Maalaea Rd., Maalaea. 808-270-7000. www.mauio ceancenter.com. Open Sept–Jun daily 9am–5pm. Jul & Aug daily 9am–6pm. $24 adults, $17 children (ages 3–12).

If your kids agree with Sebastian the Crab (from the Disney® hit *The Little Mermaid*) that "everything's bettah down where it's wettah," they'll love this place. The state-of-the-art aquarium puts little ones in the center of a giant fishbowl, where tiger sharks glide past and spotted eagle rays swoop through a 750,000-gallon tank. The **Living Reef** houses live corals and teems with moray eels, reef fish, sharks, octopi and more. Outdoor pools are home to sea turtles, tide-pool

Manta rays in Maui Ocean Center

Whales on the Cheap

You can see whales without spending a dime at McGregor Point *(mile marker 9 on Hwy. 30)* in Lahaina, in the shallow waters directly offshore. Look for the beasts as they migrate past the island's west coast. Want to learn more about these gentle giants? Take a peek at the **Whalers Village Museum** in Kaanapali to see whaling artifacts, weapons, ship models, scrimshaw, and a way-cool sperm whale skeleton *(2435 Kaanapalai Pkwy., in Whalers Village; 808-661-5992; www.whalersvillage. com/museum; open year-round daily 9:30am–10pm).*

creatures and stingrays, while the Marine Mammal Discovery Center lures kids with the eerie song of the humpback. Check out the life-size models of monk seals, dolphins and whales found in Hawaiian waters, and don't miss Hammerhead Harbor.

Hawaii Nature Center

87 Iao Valley Rd., Wailuku. 808-244-6500. Open daily 10am–4pm. $6 adults, $4 children.

Walk the short trail to the iconic **Iao Needle ★★** *(see p64)* and then let the kids loose on the 30 hands-on natural science exhibits here.

FOR KIDS

Hawaii Tourism Japan

PERFORMING ARTS

With two theaters, gallery space, and an outdoor stage, the Maui Arts and Cultural Center always has something going on that will grab you.

Maui Arts and Cultural Center

1 Cameron Way, off Kahului Beach Rd., Kahului. Box office: 808-242-7469. www.mauiarts.org. Box office open Mon–Sat, 10am–6pm. Performance times and ticket prices vary.

Diana Krall and the Mark Morris Dance Group are among the acts who have recently appeared at this state-of-the-art performance space/visual-arts gallery. It is best

Maui Arts and Cultural Center

Brigitta L. House/Michelin

known as a showcase for world music and arts, and is a good venue to catch the hottest acts in local theater and dance.

SHOPPING

The island has more than 50 galleries and a thriving community of artists. Discover cool finds (and killer donuts) in Makawao.

🏝Lahaina★★

Front Street, the main drag in downtown Lahaina, is chock-a-block with shops. Need a pair of rubber slippahs (local lingo for flip-flops), a plumeria-scented candle, or surfer gear? It's all here, and then some. Yes, there's a huge amount of cheesy stuff—loads of

T-shirts, and lots of questionable craft items made elsewhere—but if you're willing to put in some effort, you'll turn up some gems. **Maui Hands** *(612 Front St.; also in Makawao, Paia and Kaanapali)* boasts a collection created solely by Maui-based artists. Items range from Christmas ornaments to tables carved from koa wood (for a cool $10,000.)

Makawao

From Route 36 (Hana Highway), take Route 365 South 5mi to Makawao.

Formerly a rough-and-tumble paniolo (cowboy) town, Makawao's Western storefonts are

Shop in Lanai

Brigitta L. House/Michelin

now home to galleries, shops and eateries. Baldwin Avenue is a fun shopping zone with a New Age tilt. Fortify yourself with a donut-on-a-stick from Komoda Bakery, and check out the Western-wear-with-attitude at Aloha Cowboy (including handbags made from cowboy boots!) Good gallery stops include Viewpoints, David Warren, and Hot Island Glass.

Paia★

Located 7mi east of the Kahului Airport on the Hana Hwy.

A former plantation town, Paia, (say *pah-EE-ah*) has evolved into a bohemian beach hangout, a place with small boutiques and natural-food shops. Where else on the islands can you find **Hemp House**, a shop specializing in hemp goods *(16 Baldwin Ave.)* with a T-shirt whose graphics read "good bush" (a marijuana plant) and "bad bush" (George W.?)

The town makes a fun place to wander, even if the shops keep irregular hours. ("When the wind is right at Hookipa, everybody takes off," is how one local explained it.) Try **Paia Mercantile** *(corner of Hana Hwy. & Baldwin Ave.)* for pottery and art glass; **Nuage Bleu** *(76 Hana Hwy.)* for trendy girlie duds from Trina Turk, Ella Moss, Paige Denim and Juicy Couture;

Necklace, Paia Mercantile

Paia Mercantile

Maui Crafts Guild *(43 Hana Hwy.)* a cooperative gallery featuring the work of 21 artists; and **Maui Girl Beachwear** *(12 Baldwin Ave.)*, for the tiniest bikinis imaginable. Follow your nose to **Cakewalk Paia Bakery** *(corner of Hana Hwy. & Baldwin Ave.)* for their famous sinful cinnamon rolls—positively *ono* (delicious)!

Island Soap & Candle Works

Maalaea Harbor Shopping Village (next to Maui Ocean Center). 877-610-7627. www.mauisoap works.com.

Botanical products are huge on Maui—not surprising, considering the agricultural bounty of the island and the local emphasis on health and wellness. You'll find body lotions and potions made with local herbs and flowers in nearly every shop, but you know

Surf Shops

You'll find surf shops all over Maui. A couple of the best known are **Maui Tropix** *(90 Hana Hwy., Kahului; 808-871-8726)*, the exclusive dealer of Maui Built gear *(boards, tees, sunglasses, etc.)*; and **Neil Pryde Maui** *(400 Hana Hwy., Kahului; 808-321-7443; www.neilprydemaui.com)*. Once a windsurfer shop, Neil Pryde has expanded into a water sports superstore, catering to surfers and kiteboarders as well as the windsurfing crowd.

The Shops at Wailea

Brigitta L. House/Michelin

it's locally made when you watch them do it here! Master soap and candle-makers mix up batches of natural soaps, candles and bath salts. Most enticing are the super-gentle soaps, made with kukui- and macadamia-nut oils and cured for 21 days or more; the pineapple-scented bar will give you a wonderful whiff of Hawaii when you're showering back home.

Maui Swap Meet

Puunene Ave., next to Kahului Post Office, Kahului. Open Sat 7am–noon. 808-877-3100. $.50.

Forget the strip malls—do your shopping here, where you can find all sorts of trash and treasures, from vintage muumuus to hand-made jewelry.

The Shops at Wailea

3750 Wailea Alanui Dr., Wailea. 808-891-6770. www.shopsat wailea.com. Free shuttles run from Wailea resort hotels to the Shops at Wailea every 30 minutes.

Maui's most glamorous shopping address features more than 60 shops and restaurants, plus gallery receptions and live entertainment (on Wednesday). The list of galleries in the mix is truly impressive—ten, at last count—ranging from **Celebrites** (where you can find artwork created by David

Maui's Gallery Scene

Everybody knows about the island's wet-and-wild outdoor scene, but Maui isn't all surfer dudes and babes in bikinis. Surprise: the island has a high concentration of art galleries, more than 50 in all, and an active, thriving community of artists. Their work turns up in some surprising places, too, like outdoor fairs, upscale resort shopping villages, and artists' cooperatives in towns like Paia and Makawao.

Brigitta L. House/Michelin

Always in Style: The Aloha Shirt

Say "Aloha" to Hawaii's favorite shirt. Even the stuffiest of offices observes "Aloha Friday" when the colorful shirts come out to play. Vintage models from the 1930s and 40s, with real coconut buttons, are collectibles, worth thousands of dollars. The earliest Hawaiian shirts were made for plantation workers, evolving in the 1920s into wild floral designs. With the birth of rayon, the dazzlingly hued, tropical-themed garments became a must-have souvenir for the cruise-ship crowd. Now, thanks to laser technology, those old designs are new again, and hotter than ever.

Bowie, John Lennon and the like) to **Ki'i Gallery**, where the glass octopi by Dennis Mullen of Soul Glass are among one of the largest collections of studio art glass in Hawaii. **Martin & MacArthur** is the place to go for that ultimate Maui souvenir, a koa wood box or bowl. Here, **Tommy Bahama** co-exists happily with **Tiffany & Co**, and you can even find an outpost of Hawaii's answer to a general store, **ABC Stores**, which stocks everything from Hawaiian jewelry to hula dolls for your dashboard (*www.abcstores.com*).

Whalers Village

2435 Kaanapali Pkwy., Kaanapali. 808-661-4567. www.whalers village.com. Free shuttle to Whalers Village operates daily throughout the Kaanapali Beach resort area.

You can shop for surfer duds with sand between your toes—that's the beauty of Whalers Village, a real shopping destination set on Maui's most famous beach. There's a whaling museum here, too, with a giant whale skeleton as a centerpiece but, really, it's all about the shopping. Some of these

names, like **Coach** and **Louis Vuitton**, you can certainly find elsewhere, but, hey, you can't beat the ambience!

For more unique goods, check out the batik designs at **Blue Ginger** and **Blue Ginger Kids**, the dancing dolphin pendants (accented with Tahitian black pearls) at **Jessica's Gems**, the too-cute hula-girl tote bags at **Sand People**, and island-made koa bowls, Ni'ihau shell jewelry, and more at **Totally Hawaiian**.

Special Events – Whalers Village is also the place to go for fun free events, like lei-making, hula lessons and dance performances. Events calendars are posted throughout Whalers Village as well as on their website *(see left)*.

Whalers Village

Brigitta L. House/Michelin

NIGHTLIFE

Want to know who's playing where? Pick up a free copy of *Maui Time Weekly*, which provides loads of entertainment listings (www.mauitime.com).

Mulligans on the Blue

100 Kaukahi St., Wailea. 808-874-1131. www.muligansontheblue.com.

South Maui's premier party spot features a weekly line-up of live entertainment, including island contemporary music (Mon), blues and folk (Tue), sketch comedy (Thu), and traditional Irish music(!) on Sat and Sun. The crowd changes accordingly, but it's always a fun, lively vibe.

Jacques Northshore

130 Hana Hwy., Paia. 808-579-8844.

Impossibly young and buff, the local windsurfing crowd hangs here, under a canopy of colorful umbrellas. The place serves dinner, and a host of tasty appetizers (including a good, spicy ahi roll), but it's really all about the music—and the beer.

Old Lahaina Lu'au

1287 Front St., Lahaina. 808-667-1998. www.oldlahainaluau.com. $96; $65 (kids).

Unlike most luau shows, this cultural performance and feast wins high praise for authenticity. Sitting on fiber mats, you'll dine on a (really excellent) buffet featuring traditional Kalua roast pig. As the sun sets over the ocean, the show begins—a cultural journey of ancient hula, chants and music.

Casanova Italian Restaurant & Deli

118 Makawao Ave., Makawao. 808-572-0220. www.casanovamaui.com. Cover charge $7–$10.

This upscale restaurant really heats up after 10pm on weekends, when a live band or hot DJ rocks the house until 2am. Ladies' Night (Wed) is a local institution.

Early Hawaiian Music

The first musical instruments on the islands were simple wooden drums, covered with sharkskin. Dancers held small stones between their fingers and clicked them, and they tied coconut shells to their arms and legs and tapped them with sticks to create percussion. The earliest wind instruments were bamboo flutes and conch shells! Storytellers chanted poems and myths while the music played.

SPAS

Oh, the things they can do with coffee beans, volcanic clay, and Hawaiian honey! Your body never had it so good. Even better, when it's all over and you're in post-spa bliss-out mode, you're still in Maui!

Honua Spa

Hotel Hana-Maui, 5021 Hana Hwy., Hana. 808-270-5290. www.hotelhanamaui.com

Named after the Hawaiian word for 'earth,' Honua Spa takes tranquility to the next level—sheer bliss. Can't decide between a massage and a facial? You won't have to; the Honua Rainforest Mist Facial & Massage combines the two. They also offer an invigorating Hawaiian ginger body scrub, a Maui seaweed facial, and a body mask with volcanic clay. The outdoor Watsu pool, where you float in a therapist's arms, makes you feel "reborn," as one happy guest put it.

Spa Grande
© Grand Wailea Resort

Spa Grande

Grand Wailea Resort, 3850 Wailea Alanui Dr., Wailea. 800-772-1933. www.grandwailea.com.

A typical spa experience here begins with a one-hour termé Wailea hydrotherapy session—meaning, you choose a pool, perhaps an aromatic bath or a coconut milk soak. Next comes the really hard part, choosing from more than 100 treatments. Many incorporate local ingredients: there's a seashell massage, a volcanic ash facial, and a coco-java body scrub, for example. The latter features a gooey medley that smells good enough to eat: freshly ground coffee beans and Hawaiian honey, followed by a mango-coconut-latté moisturizer. Try the deep shiatsu barefoot massage, wherein a therapist walks on your back.

Spa Kea Lani

Fairmont Kea Lani Maui, 4100 Wailea Alanui Dr., Wailea. 808-875-4100 or 800-257-7544. www.fairmont.com.

Suffering from the effects of too much sun? They know just what to do at Spa Kea Lani: a gentle application of aloe and native ti leaves. Facials are absolutely irresistible here, especially the Awapuhi-chai treatment that uses organic mud scented with gingered chai, sure to leave you happily aglow.

KAUAI★★★

This lush tropical island is home to rainforests, waterfalls, sparkling sand beaches, towering sea cliffs and 5,148-foot Mount Waialeale. Visitor information: 800-262-1400 or www.kauaidiscovery.com.

Grand and diverse, Kauai is the big sister of the Hawaiian Islands, the oldest and fourth largest of the main islands.

Lush fields of greenery and thick rain forests spill down from **Mt. Waialeale**, the island's central peak, earning Kauai the nickname, "The Garden Isle."

The rain that falls on the 5,148-foot peak of Mt. Waialeale feeds seven rivers, including the state's only navigable river, and produces an on-going show of gushing waterfalls.

A deep cleft runs across the western end of the island, creating the impressive **Waimea Canyon★★**, nicknamed the "Grand Canyon of the Pacific" *(see p87)*. The stunning **Na Pali Coast★★★** *(see p85)*, with its 2,700-foot sea cliffs, lies on Kauai's northwest coast. Backpackers flock here to hike the strenuous, 11-mile **Kalalau Hiking Trail★★★**, considered one of the finest short hiking trails in the world *(see p97)*.

Fast Facts
- Kauai is home to some 62,000 people.
- The 533-square-mile island measures 33 miles long and 25 miles wide at its widest point.
- Most of Kauai's land—97 percent—has been set aside for conservation and agriculture.
- Mt. Waialeale, located roughly in the middle of the island, is one of the wettest spots on earth, with an average annual rainfall of 444 inches.
- No building on Kauai is permitted to be more than four stories high.

Indeed, Kauai claims more hiking trails than any other island.

If your idea of Hawaiian paradise is lounging on tropical beaches, don't despair. Kauai's southern and western sides are sunny and dry, and ringed with pretty stretches of warm, white sand. In fact, Kauai is home to 43 beaches—some 50 miles—more beach per mile

Aerial view of fields in Kauai

©Jiang Chen/Bigstockphoto.com

of coastline than any of the other islands. Added bonus: all of them are public.

Most of Kauai's residents now live along the Coconut Coast on the east shoreline, including **Lihue**, Kauai's main town, **Wailua**, and **Kapaa**. Tourist services cluster around three island resort areas: Lihue, sunny **Poipu** on the south shore, and the **Princeville** and **Hanalei Bay** areas on the north shore. The west side has quaint old-fashioned plantation-style towns, including charming Waimea and Hanapepe.

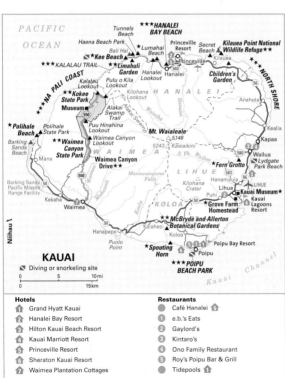

KAUAI

⊠ Diving or snorkeling site

0   5   10mi
0   15km

Hotels	Restaurants
🏠 Grand Hyatt Kauai	🔵 Café Hanalei 🏠
🏠 Hanalei Bay Resort	① e.b.'s Eats
🏠 Hilton Kauai Beach Resort	② Gaylord's
🏠 Kauai Marriott Resort	③ Kintaro's
🏠 Princeville Resort	④ Ono Family Restaurant
🏠 Sheraton Kauai Resort	⑤ Roy's Poipu Bar & Grill
🏠 Waimea Plantation Cottages	🔵 Tidepools 🏠

KAUAI

BEACHES

Kauai has more accessible beaches than any other Hawaiian island. In fact, all beaches on Kauai, from broad swaths of white sand to tiny, hidden coves, are open to the public. Even private, fancy resorts provide public access walkways to the beach.

Hanalei Bay Beach★★★

North shore, off Hwy. 560. Any road off Hwy. 560 will take you to the water.

This large, classically beautiful half-moon-shape beach is one of the most popular on Kauai's north shore. The curving crescent of white sand sits at the base of picturesque mountains—some call it the most scenic beach in Hawaii. It's tough to argue the point. Hanalei, featuring a series of three beaches strung along a too-blue-to-be-true bay, offers a bit of everything. The western end features the calmest waters, while the center of the bay boasts the highest surf, luring the island's top wave riders. You can walk the entire stretch; there are picnic areas, restrooms, and showers along the way.

Want to Know a Secret?

For your own private slice of sand head to **Secret Beach**. You'll share this golden stretch of sand with a handful of locals on a busy day; walk down the beach toward the Kilauea Lighthouse, and you'll have even more privacy.

Public nudity is against the law in Hawaii, but you may find some flaunting it here. To get there, take Kalihiwai Road, off Highway 56, a half-mile west of Kilauea.

Turn right onto the first dirt road and follow it to the parking lot at the end. The trail to the beach is easy to spot.

For a special treat, visit Hanalei Bay in the early morning, when the flat shimmering waters mirror the surrounding mountains. Hanalei Beach Park, near the east end, is a good spot for sunset viewing.

Aerial view of Halalei Bay and Kee Beaches

Hawaii Tourism Japan

Hawaii Tourism Authority/ Tor Johnson

Poipu Beach

Poipu Beach Park★★★

South shore, off Poipu Rd.

Located on the sunny, dry side of Kauai, this hard-to-resist beach is consistently ranked as one of the top in the nation. It has everything going for it: fine, white sands, tropical trade winds, and a range of water conditions to keep swimmers, snorkelers and surfers all blissfully content.

The beach actually consists of a string of three white crescents of sand, running from the Sheraton Kauai Resort east to Poipu Beach Park. Surfers and boogie boarders head to the rocky outcroppings to ride offshore breaks (rentals and lessons are available from small beachside concessions). Families and bathers stick to the east side of the rock jetty, where the relative absence of surf makes for calm waters. It's easy to make a day of it here; popular Poipu Beach Park has showers, lifeguards and picnic areas. It's also one of the fastest growing areas on the island, and you'll find a wide range of new lodging and dining choices, along with small shops and tour operators.

Spouting Horn★ – If you're in the Poipu Beach area on the southern tip of Kauai, stop to see the Spouting Horn, Kauai's answer

Monk Seals

If you're lucky, you may walk out on the beach one morning to find a Hawaiian monk seal basking in the sand. The Hawaiian monk seal remains one of the most endangered species on earth; there are only about 1,200 left that call the waters and beaches of Hawaii home. Stay at

least 100 feet away; when taking pictures, leave the flash off, and never shout or throw things at the seals in order to make them move. For more information, visit www.kauaimonkseal.com.

Hawaii Tourism Japan

BEACHES

to western geysers. The frothy surf gushes under a lava tube, and then bursts through a small opening at the surface. Sprays can reach up to 50 feet in the air, especially on windy days. At dusk, the warm-colored rays of the setting sun paint the spray in a rainbow of colors.

Kee Beach★
North shore, at the end of Hwy. 560.

Kee Beach

Hawaii Tourism Authority/Tor Johnson

the famed **Kalalau Trail★★** *(see p97)* along the **Na Pali Coast★★★** *(see p85)*. Looming to your left, as you approach the shoreline, is the impressive 1,280-foot-tall sea cliff dubbed Bali Hai, as it was known in the movie **South Pacific**. Bring your snorkeling gear; you'll spot neon-colored tropical fish as they dart around the reef toward the right side of the cove. Restrooms and showers are located near the parking lot.

Polihale Beach★
West shore, off Hwy. 50. Take Hwy. 50 west from Waimea, all the way to the end of the paved road. Continue straight on the dirt road to Polihale. The state park is at the north end of the beach. Queen's Pond, with calmer waters for swimming, is located at the south end.

Stand on the sweeping dunes of this vast, expansive beach, looking out into the wild surf, and you'll think you've been transported back in time. It's hard to imagine that beaches like this still exist in America: miles of golden sand, rugged dunes—and you won't have to fight the crowds!

The isolated, golden beach, stretching 17 miles, is the state's longest and one of its most serene and picturesque. (**Warning:** the surf can be dangerous.) Granted, Polihale Beach is a bit difficult to get to, resting on the westernmost point on the island down a long, dirt road, but it's worth the trek. According to Hawaiian mythology, Polihale was the gateway to the Afterworld, drawing spirits and ghosts to its shores.

After resting, the spirits would climb the towering sea cliffs and leap off to get to Po, the offshore Afterworld. Polihale means "House of Po." **Polihale State Park** sits at the northern end of the beach, equipped with restrooms, showers and picnic areas.

PARKS AND NATURAL SITES

Discover cloud-shrouded mountains, misty rain forests, sea cliffs, caves, blowholes, fern grottos, canyons and more.

Na Pali Coast★★★

Begins at the end of the road at Kee Beach, on Kauai's northwest coast.

The 22-mile stretch of rugged and remote coastline along Kauai's northwest shores is arguably one of the most beautiful natural spots on earth. Known the world over, the Na Pali Coast, stretching from Kee Beach in the north to Polihale State Park in the west, has inspired poets, artists and photographers for thousands of years. It's also been the backdrop for several movies *(see box, above right)*. Some historians believe that this area was the first to be settled in Kauai by the early Hawaiians. Today, it is only accessible by the strenuous **Kalalau Hiking Trail★★★** *(see p97)*, guided boat or kayak trips (several outfitters

Pretty as a Picture

It's no surprise that many people get an eerie sense of *déjà vu* when they land in Kauai; after all, the island has been a favorite of Hollywood filmmakers for decades. In all, Kauai has served as the backdrop for more than 60 major movies and television shows, including the beachy, island scenes in *South Pacific*, the wedding scene in *Blue Hawaii*, the opening waterfall shot in *Jurassic Park*, and the jungle scenes in *Outbreak*.

offer Na Pali Coast excursions), or viewed from a helicopter *(see p95)*. No matter how you see the dramatic coastline—with its soaring sea cliffs, hanging valleys, gushing waterfalls, sea caves, lava tubes and pristine beaches—you won't be disappointed. Make sure you have plenty of film or an extra battery pack for this excursion!

Hawaii Tourism Japan

Na Pali Coast

Views of the Kalalau Valley, Kokee State Park

Hawaii Tourism Authority/Ron Dahlquist

Kokee State Park★★

Off Hwy. 550, 15mi north of Kekaha. 808-241-3444. www.hawaii.stateparks.org. Open year-round daily dawn–dusk.

Had enough of hot, dry weather? Head to this cool, mountainous park on the far west end of Kauai. On your way there, you'll have several great views of Waimea Canyon *(see p87)*. Once in the park, there are not-to-be-missed lookouts across the deep Kalalau Valley, plunging to the remote Na Pali Coast *(see p85)*. The 4,345-acre park features forests of koa and red-blossoming ohia lehua trees, and a spiderweb of rippling streams. On clear days, you may have views of rainy Mt. Waialeale and below to Alakai Swamp.

Kokee Natural History Museum *– Located at mile marker 15. 808-335-9975. www.kokee.org. Open year-round daily 10am–4pm.* Stop by this tiny museum, located at the park headquarters, to check out the displays of ancient artifacts and local plants.

Hiking in the Park – There are 45 miles of trails to explore in Kokee State Park, from easy nature walks to strenuous day hikes. Most offer fabulous views across the rugged Kauai interior. Pick up trail maps at the Kokee Natural History Museum.

- The short **Nature Trail** near the museum offers a quick stretch of the legs and a look at native plants.
- One of the most popular hikes in the park, the **Pihea Trail** *(3.5mi one way; allow 4 hours; trailhead located about 4mi past museum)* traverses a high ridge between the Kalalau Valley and the Alakai Swamp, with sweeping views of valley cliffs dropping to the ocean.
- If you're up for a challenge (and don't mind getting muddy and wet!), try the **Alakai Swamp**

Cabins for Rent

If you're looking for an economical place to stay, close to hiking trails and fabulous mountain scenery, check into the cabins for rent at Kokee State Park. The Lodge at Kokee operates 12 cabins, each sleeping up to six people. The older cabins feature one room with bunk beds, kitchen and bath. Newer cabins have two bedrooms, a living area, kitchen and bath. All come equipped with bed linens and cooking utensils. You can rent the cabins year-round, but make sure you reserve months in advance *(contact the Lodge at Kokee, PO Box 367, Waimea, HI 96796; 808-355-6061; www.thelodgeatkokee.net).*

- **Trail**. The mossy 3.5-mile path cuts through thick rain forests and swampy bogs before reaching Kilohana Lookout.

Waimea Canyon State Park★★

11mi north of Kekaha on Hwy. 550 (Kokee Rd.). 808-274-3444 (information) or 808-245-6001 (weather conditions). www.hawaiistateparks.org. Open year-round daily dawn–dusk.

Mark Twain called it the "Grand Canyon of the Pacific." Although it measures some ten miles long, one mile wide, and more than 3,500 feet deep, it's not only the size that's impressive about Waimea Canyon (the largest in the Pacific)—it's also the colors. The deeply scarred canyon walls, carved from rivers that pour down

Touring Tip
Don't waste your time driving around the perimeter of Kauai to find "Barking Sands," even though playful locals might urge you to go see them! Barking Sands is not a natural wonder, but the name of a military installation and missile range. Perhaps the sands really do bark, but you'll have to get past security in order to investigate!

from Mt. Waialeale's wet summit, shimmer and shine in the sunlight like a palette of deep-hued jewels. Emerald-green folds and rugged dark cliffs plunge into the rust-colored rivers below. On clear days (mornings are the best times), you may see waterfalls and rainbows against the eons-old volcanic rock. There are several lookout points along the **Waimea Canyon**

Anne Austin/Michelin

Waimea Canyon

Don't Feed the Birds
If you're hungry, the lodge next door to the Kokee Natural History Museum *(see p86)* serves breakfast and lunch. Just don't feed the local jungle fowl that often congregate in the area. They may look like chickens but they're actually moa, brought over to the islands by early Polynesians. Today, moa live only on Kauai, the only island free of the mongoose, which loves to eat moa eggs for breakfast.

PARKS AND NATURAL SITES

87

Fern Grotto

Hawaii Tourism Authority/Kirk Lee Aeder

Drive★★ *(see p89)*, and the canyon is accessible for hiking, camping and fishing. Check in with the staff at **Kokee State Park★★** headquarters *(see p86)*, which also administers **Waimea Canyon State Park★★**, for information on recreational activities in and around the canyon.

Fern Grotto★

Off Hwy. 56 in Wailua Marina State Park. 866-482-9775. www.ferngrottokauai.com. Boat rentals and guided excursions to the grotto are available at the Marina Section off Kuhio Hwy. (Hwy. 56.)

It's too bad you can't have this pretty place to yourself: a lava-rock cave heavily draped in tropical ferns, set along the historic Wailua River. Alas, misty Fern Grotto is one of Kauai's most popular attractions and, some say, a bit too commercialized. Rental boats, kayaks, pleasure boats and guided pontoons ply the Wailua River on their way to the grotto. It's a popular spot for weddings, too. Join the crowds on a guided trip, where you'll see historic sites, tropical gardens and waterfalls.

Kayak and Boat Tours
Rainbow Kayak – *866-826-2505 or 866-826-9983, www.rainbowkayak.com.*
Kayak Wailua – *808-822-3388. www.kayakwailua.com.*
Smith's Tropical Paradise – *808-821-6895. www.smithskauai.com.* Smith's offers guided boat tours to the grotto, along with nightly luaus.

A Place for the Birds
Bird watchers flock to the **Kilauea Point National Wildlife Refuge**, off Kuhio Highway *(Hwy. 56)* on the north shore of Kauai *(see p100)*. The refuge, overlooking rugged sea cliffs and Kilauea Bay, is home to nesting red-footed boobies (Feb–Aug), laysan albatrosses (Nov–Jun), wedge-tailed shearwaters (Apr–Oct) and red-tailed tropicbirds (Mar–Sept). Look for great frigate birds that come here to feed, and for the endangered nene bird *(see p62)*. You'll also have fine views of the northern coastline from the refuge.

SCENIC DRIVES

Everywhere you go in Kauai is a scenic drive, with views of waterfalls, misty mountains, pretty coves and sandy beaches. *See map p81.*

Waimea Canyon Drive★★

Begin in Waimea, on Hwy. 50, on the southwest coast of Kauai. See p87.

Waimea Canyon is one of Hawaii's most dramatic sites. The ten-mile-long, one-mile-wide, 3,500-foot-deep canyon, the largest in the Pacific, offers majestic views akin to Arizona's Grand Canyon. Schedule a half-day for this excursion, more if you plan on doing one of the hikes in **Kokee State Park★★**.

Head west on Highway 50 to the town of **Waimea**, a good place to stop for picnic makings to take with you on the drive through the canyon. You'll pass the small Captain Cook Monument (the British explorer landed in Waimea Bay in 1778), before reaching Kokee Road (Hwy. 550) heading up to the canyon. As the narrow road climbs through wild sugarcane fields, look back toward the southeast for glimpses of the blue ocean with its streaks of frothy, white surf.

Lookouts – Stop at **Waimea Canyon Lookout** for sweeping views of the plunging 3,500-foot-high walls and a kaleidoscope of multihued ridges. Below, the Waimea River shimmers, snaking through the lush valley, and waterfalls tumble down the canyon like shiny silver ribbons. Continue on to **Puu Hinahina Lookout**, where, on clear days, you can look out to the ocean and the island of Niihau, 17 miles southwest of Kauai. There's also another fine view of the canyon from here.

Follow Highway 550 to the **Kokee Natural History Museum** and park headquarters *(see p86)*, and stop to pick up information about the canyon, local flora and fauna, and hiking trails in **Kokee State Park★★** *(see p86)*.

View from Kalalau Lookout in Waimea Canyon State Park

©Photo75/iStockphoto.com

SCENIC DRIVES

You'll be tempted to turn around here, but don't. Continue to the end of the road and you'll discover two more fine views of the rugged sea cliffs of the **Na Pali Coast★★★** *(see p85)* along the way at the **Kalalau** and **Pulu o Kila lookouts.**

As you head back on your return trip, look for Makaha Ridge Road. You'll find it between mile markers 13 and 14 along Highway 550, near the Puu Hinahina Lookout. This is a great alternative return route. The road drops a dramatic 2,000 feet to the Pacific Ocean, with forest and valley views along the way. Makaha Ridge Road ends at the Pacific Tracking Station, part of the Pacific Range Facility owned by the US. Army. You'll find a nice oceanfront picnic area nearby.

North Shore★★★

Begin in the town of Kapaa on Kauai's east coast and take the Kuhio Hwy. (Hwy. 56) north.

Verdant taro fields, cloud-shrouded mountains, tumbling waterfalls, postcard-perfect tropical beaches, rain forests, rivers and rugged sea cliffs await visitors who travel the narrow, winding roads and one-lane bridges of Kauai's pristine north shore. Save some time to explore Kapaa, a pleasant 19th-century plantation town. There's plenty of shopping in town, including the open air **Coconut Marketplace** *(see p101)*. If you have time, you may also want to take a walking tour of the town, led by the **Kauai Historical Society**. The 90-minute tours highlight the town's history and unique architecture. If the wind is blowing and the waves are up, consider a walk on Kapaa Beach, a popular hangout with local surfers. Before heading north, take a side trip to view pretty Opaekaa Falls on the north branch of Wailua River. From Kuhio Highway, take Kuamoo Road (next to Coco Palms Resort) for two miles. You'll find a turnout on the right and a scenic overlook for the falls. Now, head north on the Kuhio Highway. If you've timed it right: stop by the 240-acre **Na Aina Kai Botanical Gardens** in Kilauea *(4101 Waiiapa Rd., 808-828-0575; www.naainakai.com)*. The gardens,

Taro field in Hanalei Valley

Hawaii Tourism Japan

Shrimp Shacks and Plate Lunches

A favorite stop along Highway 50 on Kauai's western shore is the tiny Shrimp Shack in Waimea *(south side of Hwy. 50, in the town center)*. Order up a heaping plate of fresh coconut-battered Kauai shrimp, with hand-cut spicy fries and cold lemonade to go. Or, stop by the West Kauai Craft Fair *(south side of Hwy. 50, in the center of Waimea)*, where a local vendor serves classic Hawaiian-style plate lunches, platters of barbecue chicken, marinated pork or salmon, with sides of rice and cabbage. He's there every Saturday and Sunday from about noon to 5pm. Then, browse the open-air stands of locally made crafts, including jewelry, art and wood products.

including 12 theme gardens, a hardwood plantation, a moss-and-fern draped canyon, and a sandy beach along the ocean, are open by guided tour only *(Tue, Wed & Thu at 9am, 9:30am & 1pm.)* There's also a fun-filled Children's Garden, where kids can roam through a gecko-shaped maze of bushes and plants, and climb a treehouse. Farther up the road is the **Kilauea Point National Wildlife Refuge**★★ *(see p100).* Located on the northernmost point of the Hawaiian Islands, the oceanside preserve features a 1913 lighthouse, overlooking the crashing surf. This is a favorite spot for bird-watchers (look for soaring frigates and red-footed boobies.) Back on the highway, you'll pass the ultra-luxe Princeville Resort *(see p182),* before reaching the beautiful Hanalei Lookout.

Hawaii Tourism Japan

Kilauea Point National Wildlife Refuge

Java Stop

The friendly town of **Hanalei** is a good place to stop for replenishment. There's a small shopping center with a cluster of craft and souvenir shops, and a handful of good restaurants. **Java Kai** *(5-5183C Kuhio Hwy.; 808-808-826-6717)* serves up breakfast and a great cup of coffee. Hit the **Aloha Juice Bar** for fresh smoothies *(this mobile juice bar is parked in the lot of Old Ching Young Center, 5-5190 Kuhio Hwy, 808-826-6990)*, and the **Polynesian Café** *(5-5190 Kuhio Hwy., in the Old Ching Young Center; 808-826-1999)* for pork sandwiches, stir-frys, and fresh fish-and-chip baskets.

Lappert's Ice Cream – Stop the Car!

Keep your eyes peeled for the yellow and red **Lappert's Ice Cream** sign, and pull over fast when you see it *(1-3555 Kaumualii Hwy., Hanapepe; 808-335-6121)*. Lappert's super-rich Kauai-made ice cream (it contains 16- to 18 percent butterfat) is flavored with fresh island ingredients. Try Kauai pie, a decadent mixture of Kona coffee ice cream, chunky macadamia nuts, coconut and chocolate fudge, piled into a large waffle cone; or go for guava cheesecake, mango, Poha berry, banana fudge... so many flavors, so little time.

Be sure to stop here for views of the luxuriant, ancient taro fields that spread across the valley. It's one of the finest views on Kauai and one of its most photographed vistas.

As you continue west, you'll have views of flat pasturelands (and a few grazing horses), bumping up against the folded mountain range.

Heading west out of town, there are pretty views of **Hanalei Bay★★★** and its crescent-shape beaches (see p82), as the road slices through mountains laced with waterfalls on one side and the turquoise-hued ocean on the other. There are a number of

Island-style Souvenirs

When touring the island, be on the lookout for local galleries, shops, and roadside markets, where you're likely to find the best souvenirs and unique reminders of your visit to the islands. One idea: look for body products made with local ingredients (lavender oils, kukui nut cream). Here are a few suggestions for other made-in-Hawaii souvenirs:

- Aloha shirts and surf shorts
- Lau hala placemats
- Woodcrafts (koa mirrors, picture frames, ukuleles)
- CDs by local island musicians.

pullouts and overlooks along the way, including **Lumahai Beach★**, made famous by Mitzi Gaynor in the movie *South Pacific*.

The pretty, white-sand beach, flanked by lava rocks, is fine for a stroll but don't try swimming here. There are very strong currents and rip tides that make it unsafe most of the time.

Next you'll pass **Tunnels Beach**, where deep, offshore caverns and a large reef make it a prime spot for diving and snorkeling, and **Haena Beach Park**, popular with locals and campers.

You'll reach pretty **Kee Beach★** *(see p84)* and the start of the **Na Pali Coast★★★** *(see p85)* at the end of the road. Take a refreshing swim in the balmy, gentle waters here; it's also a good place for snorkeling, around the reef toward the right side of the cove.

The backdrop is postcard-perfect, with sea cliffs and tropical forests. To your right as you approach the shoreline, is the impressive 1, 280-foot-tall sea cliff, named Bali Hai in the movie *South Pacific*.

Still have energy and time? Consider a short jaunt on the **Kalalau Trail★★** *(see p97)*, which begins here. Even a short walk on this spectacular trail will reward you with sweeping views of the rugged **Na Pali Coast★★★** *(see p85)*.

KAUAI

MUST SEE

GARDENS

Look around: There are lush gardens and tropical forests everywhere, including some of the top formal botanical gardens in the country.

Limahuli Garden★★

Next to the entrance of Haena State Park, off Hwy. 560, Haena. 808-826-1053. www.ntbg. org. Open year-round Tue–Sat 9:30am–4pm. $15 self-guided tour, $25 guided tour. Children under 12 free.

Located on the dramatic north shore of Kauai, Limahuli is considered one of the top botanical gardens in the US. A short loop takes you along ancient taro terraces and aside pretty Limahuli Stream, to a stunning overlook of rugged cliffs and open ocean views. The garden specializes in native Hawaiian culture and plants, encompassing more than 1,000 acres. The public gardens spill over 17 acres; the surrounding 988 acres is a nature reserve.

McBryde and Allerton Botanical Gardens★★

On Lawaii Beach Rd., across from the Spouting Horn, Poipu. 808-742-2623. www.ntbg.org. Open year-round daily 9am–4pm. Closed major holidays. McBryde: $20 self-guided tour, $40 guided tour; Allerton: guided tour only $40. Children are half-price, but minimum age is 10 years old.

These two side-by-side gardens feature impressive displays of rare and endangered tropical plants, showcased against a backdrop of shimmering pools and garden sculpture. Self-guided and guided tours are offered at the McBryde Garden. Only guided walks are available at the Allerton Gardens, where you'll see the wavy roots of the Moreton Bay fig tree, featured in the movie *Jurassic Park.*

View of irrigated terrace with taro, Limahuli Gardens

Hawaii Tourism Authority/ Tor Johnson

HISTORIC SITES

Legends and folklore surround the historic sites, including swinging bridges, ancient fish ponds, and sugar cane plantations.

Grove Farm Homestead★

Nawiliwili Rd., off Waapa Rd. near Lihue. 808-245-3202. Visit by 2-hour guided tour only, year-round Mon, Wed & Thu 10am & 1pm (reservations required). Closed major holidays. $5 adults, $2 children (ages 12 and under).

For a good look at life on an early sugar plantation, sign up for the two-hour tour of this historic homestead. Grove Farm, nestled in the pastures above Lihue, was founded in 1864 by George N. Wilcox, the son of Hanalei missionaries.

The 80-acre farm preserves the lifestyle of the sugar plantation from the period 1864 to 1978, and includes the restored Wilcox family home, plantation office and workers' houses.

On the extensive grounds, you'll discover gardens, orchards, poultry and livestock.

MUSEUMS

The Garden Isle has little to offer traditional museum-hoppers, but the tiny Kauai Museum in Lihue provides a fine overview of island history.

Kauai Museum★

4428 Rice St., Lihue. 808-245-6931. www.kauaimuseum.org. Open year-round Mon–Fri 9am–4pm, Sat 10am–4pm. $10.

You'll find all things Hawaiian at this small, but top-notch, museum in Lihue. The museum traces the island's history from its volcanic beginnings, through sugarcane farming and missionary work. It's an impressive collection of Hawaiian paintings and artifacts, including more than 1,000 stone implements, feather work, weapons, drums and more; 5,000 photographs dating from the 1890s, old plantation records and postcards; and a textile collection with 50 Hawaiian-made quilts.

Don't miss the permanent collection of Hawaiian works from well-known artists, including 30 framed oil paintings by Alfred Gurrey. There's a nice gift shop on-site, too *(see p101)*.

Kauai Museum

Kauai Museum

FOR FUN

Lofty helicopter rides, jungle ziplines, top-notch hiking, movie tours, underwater adventures and more offer non-stop fun.

Take a Helicopter Ride★★★

If you do only one thing on Kauai (besides sunbathe on the beach), make it a helicopter tour of the island.

More than 90 percent of the island's diverse and spectacular landscape is inaccessible; the best way to see it is from the air. Most tours fly out of Lihue, heading toward the sunny south shores of **Poipu★★★**, with its long stretches of sandy beaches and turquoise bays. You'll chopper over the dramatic **Waimea Canyon★★** cliffs.

If you're lucky, it will have just rained and you'll see countless, minutes-old waterfalls tumbling down the canyon walls.

Heading north, the spectacular **Na Pali Coast★★★** comes into view, with its lush cliffs, plunging 3,000 to 4,000 feet to the sea. Inaccessible by roads, this remote coastline, with its rugged cliffs and verdant valleys, was once home to thousands of ancient Hawaiians. Its jungly, primeval landscape has been seen in several movies, including *Jurassic Park*.

View of a waterfall in the Waimea Canyon from on board a helicopter

Hawaii Tourism Authority / Tor Johnson

The flight continues up the coast, passing sparkling **Hanalei Bay★★★** and a smattering of pretty beaches. If weather permits, the pilot may take you into the middle of the island's crater, once sacred burial grounds for kings, then over Mt. Waialeale, the center of the island and one of the rainiest spots on the whole earth.

Have you counted the waterfalls along the way? One young passenger got to 100, then gave up the count.

Do You Believe in Menehunes?

Hawaii folklore tells of mischievous "little people" named menehunes, who roamed the forests at night. The shy creatures, it's said, were great engineers and master builders, capable of completing major construction projects in one night. The creation of **Menehune Fishpond** and **Waimea Ditch** on Kauai are credited to the menehunes. Not just workers, these jolly folks also enjoyed singing and dancing, and have been known to use magic arrows to pierce hearts and ignite feelings of love. Some people believe that menehune still hide out in the forests of Kauai.

FOR FUN

95

Touring Tip

One of the most reputable helicopter tour operators is **Island Helicopters** *(808-245-8588 or 800-829-5999; www.islandhelicopters.com)*. For a full list of operators, contact **Kauai Visitors Bureau** *(808-245-3971 or 800-262-1400; www.kauai discovery.com)*. Online booking can save up to 40 percent.

Join a Hawaii Movie Tour

Tours run at about $120 per person and include lunch and pick-up and return from most resort properties. For more information, contact Hawaii Movie Tours: 800-628-8432; www.hawaiimovietour.com.

Even if you're not a movie buff, you'll enjoy the incredible scenery on this fun-filled tour of famous movie scenes and locations shot on Kauai. The island has long been a favorite of location scouts and filmmakers, who've shot more than six-dozen movies on the Garden Isle. On this guided tour, you'll see a variety of famous film scenes on the bus (shown on digital video with surround sound), as you tour the actual sites.

Along the way, you'll be treated to in-depth commentary, behind-the-scenes gossip, and a good amount of hilarity.

The tour visits a number of well-known public sites, like the waterfall shown in the opening scene of the TV show *Fantasy Island*, and the beach where Mitzi Gaynor vowed to "wash that man right outta my hair" in the movie *South Pacific*. But you'll also visit private locales and hidden, off-the-tourist-track spots. Remember the scene in *Raiders of the Lost Ark* where Indiana Jones was chased by a band of South American warriors, then swung on a rope to escape on a waiting seaplane? You'll visit the private ranch where it was filmed.

The rope is still hanging, and, if you like, you can take a swing on it, too, Indiana-style. (Don't tell anyone, but according to the tour guides, Harrison Ford had to have a stunt double step in to do that trick.)

Movie Tours, Inc.

Bali Hai Lookout

One of the finest views on the island of Kauai is from the opulent **Princeville Resort** on the north shore *(5520 Ka Haku Rd., Princeville; see p182)*. But you don't have to fork out the princely sum to stay here in order to soak up the views. Reserve a table at the resort's **Café Hanalei** *(see p170)* or simply pull up a chair at the poolside terrace bar. You'll have a stunning view of Hanalei Bay, the famous Bali Hai rock formation, and the cliffs of Na Molokama. Stick around as the sun slips into the water and the resort's twinkling lanterns alight.

Hike the Na Pali Coast★★★

Kalalau trailhead begins at Kee Beach at the end of Hwy. 560. Permits are required on Kalalau Trail beyond Hanakapiai Beach. Camping along the Kalalau trail costs $10 per day.

For more information, and to purchase permits, contact the Division of State Parks (PO Box 621, Honolulu, HI 96809; 808-587-0300; www.hawaiistateparks.org).

Kalalau Hiking Trail★★★

If you're a hiker, or even a quasi outdoor adventurer, you'll love this well-known trail that hugs the remote and rugged Na Pali coastline. It's arguably one of the best short-distance hikes in the world.

It's not easy. The 11-mile, one-way trek includes some 5,000 feet of elevation gain and loss, often across a narrow, steep, muddy and slippery ridgeline. But you'll be rewarded with spectacular views. On the first leg of the trip—the

Touring Tip

If you can't carve out time to do the entire trail, the first two miles to Hanakapiai Beach is worthwhile and will give you a good peek at the stunning Na Pali coastline. From here you can also make a four-mile round-trip to **Hanakapiai Falls**.

relatively easy one, though it gets slippery when wet—you'll walk through a tropical forest of dewy ferns, sweet-smelling papaya and mango trees, with sweeping ocean vistas, before descending onto sugar-white **Hanakapiai Beach**. Here, a freshwater stream bubbles into the ocean and wet and dry caves line the shoreline. Back on the Kalalau Trail, you'll climb up and down into **Hoolulu Valley**, then **Hanakoa Valley**, rich with tropical plants, mango and guava trees. The final leg takes you into breathtaking **Kalalau Valley★★**, rippled with streams and waterfalls. There's camping on the beach at Kalalau.

©Lori Spiker/Fotolia.com

Kalalau Hiking Trail

Poipu Bay Golf Course.

Grand Hyatt Kauai Resort and Spa

KAUAI

MUST DO

Camping on Kauai

You'll find some of the best camping in Hawaii on Kauai, including three state parks and several county beach parks. Cabins are available at **Kokee State Park★★** *(15mi north of Kekaha on Hwy. 550; see p86)* and backcountry permits are offered for sites in the **Waimea Canyon★★** *(11mi north of Kekaha on Hwy. 550)* and adjoining **Kokee State Park★★**. For the best beach camping, consider **Polihale State Park** *(at the end of a 5mi-long dirt road from Mana Village, off Hwy. 50)*, with its lofty sand dunes, miles of secluded beach, picnic areas and fresh water. And you can pull your vehicle right up on to the beach here!

Golf Kauai

Golfers can hardly go wrong on the island of Kauai, home to several dramatic, award-winning resort courses.

Kauai Lagoons – *3351 Hoolaulea Way, Lihue. 808-241-6000 or 800-634-6400. www.kauailagoonsgolf. com.* Kauai Lagoons boasts two Jack Nicklaus-designed courses on the southeast corner of the island, including the top-ranked Kiele course that snakes through 40 acres of tropical lagoons.

Poipu Bay – *At the Grand Hyatt Kauai Resort, 2250 Ainako St., Koloa. 800-858-6300. www.poipubaygolf. com (see p182).* A Robert Trent Jones Jr. design, the course at Poipu Bay features rolling terrain, sweeping ocean views, and a

Sunset Viewing on Kauai

It's tough not to slow down, stop and gawk at the legendary sunsets on Kauai. There are plenty of prime sunset viewing spots but for the very best, head to Polihale Beach. The three-mile stretch of mostly secluded white sand on Kauai's western coast gets bathed in sherbert-colored hues as the sun slips down past the horizon. Stick around for fabulous star gazing, too. Once a month, on the Saturday nearest the full moon, locals and visitors head to the Barking Sands Observatory near Polihale Beach to enjoy the brilliant night skies.

Hawaii Tourism Authority/ Tor Johnson

choice of four sets of tees at each hole. The PGA Grand Slam was held here from 1994 to 2006. **Princeville Resort** – *5520 Ka Haku Rd., Princeville. 800-826-1105. www. princeville.com (see p182)*. Robert Trent Jones Jr. designed both of the resort's courses. Set against a backdrop of open ocean, the 45 holes of the **Prince Course** are named for Prince Albert, the only son of King Kamehameha IV; the **Makai Course**, among the top 100 resort courses in the country, features three sets of nines that skirt the ocean and wind through tropical forest.

Kayak a Sacred River

Take a guided kayak trip up the scared Wailua River. The 20-mile-long river on Kauai's east coast (only three miles are navigable) is shrouded in mystery and mystique. Legend has it that the spirits of the dead would travel up the river to the cliffs of Haeleele, where they would jump to the next life.

The kayak-hike excursion, offered by **Kayak Kauai** *(800-437-3507 off*

Best Golf Shop

If you're a golfer, or you have duffers on your gift list, you'll want to check out **The Golf Shop at Poipu Bay Golf Course**, rated as one of the finest in America. PGA Grand Slam and Kauai Resort logo wear fly off the shelves here.

island or 808-826-9844 on Kauai; www.kayakkauai.com) begins with a 2.5-mile paddle upstream. The river is fairly gentle, and easy enough for families with young children. After about a 45-minute paddle you'll reach a landing and the trailhead to Secret Falls. The gentle one-mile trail travels through overgrown forests of mango, ginger, and tall albizia trees, before reaching the picturesque 120-foot falls. There's a small swimming hole and perfect perches for a picnic lunch.

If you prefer coastal, sea-swept views, Kayak Kauai, and a number of other local outfitters, offer sea kayaking excursions, some combining stops at prime snorkeling spots.

Hawaii Tourism Europe

Kayaking on the Wailua River

FOR KIDS

You'll find outdoor activities and non-stop adventure on laid-back and casual Kauai, arguably the family-friendliest of the Hawaiian Islands.

Go Snorkeling★★

A pair of rubber slippers and a snorkel mask (don't forget the sunscreen!) is all you'll need to catch Kauai's amazing underwater show. The best family-friendly snorkeling beaches on the island are **Poipu Beach Park★★★** *(see p83)*, Anini and Salt Pond Beach on the south shore, and **Kee Beach★** on the north shore *(see p84)*. Check out **Lydgate Park Beach** *(off Hwy. 56 between Kapaa and Lihue; take Leho Rd. past the Holiday Inn Sunspree)*, too, for great swimming, tide pooling, and snorkeling. Lydgate also has an awesome playground with a maze of caves, slides and tunnels that will keep the little ones occupied for hours.

Kilauea Point National Wildlife Refuge★★

On the north shore, off Hwy. 56; take Kilauea Rd. to the end. 808-828-1413. www.fws.gov/ kilaueapoint.

Take a hike on the wild side. Red-footed booby birds, soaring frigates, spouting humpback whales, basking monk seals and frolicking spinner dolphins are just some of the wildlife your family may see at the Kilauea Point National Wildlife Refuge, perched on a cliff overlooking the Pacific Ocean. Take a walk out to the 1913 lighthouse, stop by the visitor center for information and maps,

Alae Ula (Hawaiian Gallinule)

Hawaii Tourism Japan

then join a guided walk through the trails that crisscross the 203-acre preserve. Located on the northernmost tip of the Hawaiian Islands, Kilauea Point is one of the few Hawaiian refuges open to the public.

Head for the Backcountry★

Zippety-do-da! Don a miner's helmet and bring your sense of adventure on a zipline tour of the backcountry. Kauai Backcountry Adventures *(3-4131 Kuhio Highway. Hanama'ulu, 888-270-0555; www. kauaibackcountry.com)* takes small groups to a former 17,000-acre plantation, via four-wheel drive vehicle, and then the real fun begins! Let 'er rip on a series of seven ziplines that descend and traverse an overgrown mountainside. The scenery is lush (think: rain forests, streams, bamboo groves, and waterfalls) and the ride is exhilarating. **Note:** Kids must be at least 12 years old.

SHOPPING

The best shopping is clustered in a few marketplaces. For fresh produce and local goods, check out the island's Sunshine Markets.

Coconut Marketplace

4-484 Kuhio Hwy. (Hwy. 56), Kapaa. 808-822-3641. www.coconutmarketplace.com. Open year-round Mon–Sat 9am–9pm, Sun 10am–6pm.

This open-air marketplace, with more than 60 shops and restaurants, is the largest on Kauai. If you're looking for one-stop shopping, this is it. Here, you'll find fine specialty stores next to inexpensive gift shops, tacky souvenirs cheek-to-jowl with pricey Tahitian pearls.

Brigitta L. House/Michelin

Kauai Museum Shop

4428 Rice St., Lihue. 808-245-6931. www.kauaimuseum.org. Open year-round Mon–Fri 9am–4pm, Sat 10am–4pm. Closed Thanksgiving Day & Dec 25.

This is where the locals go to shop for special gifts. It's also the best place for top-quality, one-of-a-kind, island-made arts and crafts. An impressive selection of items awaits you at this tiny museum shop, including fish-hook necklaces, Lauhala hats, wooden bowls, and authentic Niihau shell necklaces ranging from $75 to $15,000.

Sunshine Markets★

Pick up fresh, locally grown produce at one of Kauai's farmers' markets.

Monday – noon at Koloa Ballpark *(Maluhia Rd., Koloa).*
Tuesday – 3pm at Kalaheo Neighborhood Center *(on Papalina Rd., off Kaumualii Rd., Kalaheo).*
Wednesday – 3pm at Kapaa New Town Park *(at the intersection of Kahau & Olehena Rds., Kapaa).*
Thursday – 4:30pm at Kilauea Neighborhood Center *(on Keneke Rd., off Lighthouse Rd., Kilauea);* and 3pm at Hanapepe Town Park *(behind the fire station in Hanapepe).*
Friday – 3pm at Vidinha Stadium in Lihue *(on Hoolako St., off Queen Kapuli Rd.).*
Saturday – 9am at Kekaha Neighborhood Center *(on Elepaio Rd., Kekaha).*

Kauai Made
Want to be sure your souvenir was made on Kauai? Look for the Kauai Made label. The award-winning program focuses on promoting the island's small businesses, which sell products made on Kauai or with Kauai materials. For a brochure, list and map of vendors, visit www.kauaimade.net.

SHOPPING

NIGHTLIFE

Kauai is not particularly known for its rollicking après-sun scene (moonlit walks on the beach and sunset toasts are more its style), but there are a handful of hot night spots you won't want to miss.

Keoki's Paradise

2360 Kiahuna Plantation Dr., at the Poipu Shopping Center, Koloa. 808-742-7534. www.keokisparadise.com.

This casual, lively Polynesian-themed restaurant, decked out with waterfalls, thatched roofs and plenty of plants, is a hangout for young partyers on Friday and Saturday evenings when local bands perform in the bustling Bamboo Bar. A bar menu of pupus, salads and light fare is available until 11:30pm.

Stevenson's Library

1571 Poipu Rd., Koloa. 808-742-1234. www.kauai.hyatt.com.

Sip fine liquors, play a game of chess, enjoy a hand-crafted cigar... this opulent bar in the Grand Hyatt Kauai Resort & Spa on the south shore a big-city gentlemen's club. The upscale night spot is decorated in

Moonbows

The best nightly performance on Kauai is often courtesy of Mother Nature. The Garden Isle is one of the few places in the world to see moonbows. Look for these ghostly light streaks when the moon is full, just after sunset. On the highway between Lihue and Waimea is a good place to spot them.

dark woods and brass accents, and features a 27-foot-long koa-wood bar. Sink into the cushy sofas and chairs and enjoy live jazz, offered nightly from 8pm to 11pm.

Tahiti Nui

25-5134 Kuhio Hwy., Hanalei, 808-826-6277. www.thenui.com.

If you're going to party only one night on Kauai, make it at the Tahiti Nui—or, as the locals call it "da nui." This long-standing North Shore watering hole and casual, family-owned restaurant has let the good times roll for more than five decades. Live music, just-right mai tais, and anything goes, friendly atmosphere draw locals, visitors, and celebrities alike. The beloved old-time Tiki Bar features Karoake on Thursday nights and dancing every night into the small hours.

Stevenson's Library

Grand Hyatt Kauai Resort and Spa

SPAS

You'll find a handful of day spas, popular with locals, but the most opulent and cutting edge spas are located at the large resorts.

Anara Spa

Grand Hyatt Kauai Resort and Spa

Anara Spa

Grand Hyatt Kauai, 1571 Poipu Rd., Koloa. 808-240-6440. www.anaraspa.com.

This blissful and beautiful full-service spa, set on the lush grounds of the Grand Hyatt Kauai resort *(see p182)*, is considered one of the top-ranked spas in the country. It's also the largest on Kauai and the second largest in Hawaii.

From the moment you walk through the doors, you'll feel pampered in the luxurious indoor and outdoor facilities and by the spa's unique, therapeutic treatments.

Popular treatments include the seaweed and mineral body masks, botanical baths, papaya pineapple polishes, and pohaku (hot stone) and lomilomi massages *(see box, below right)*. The outdoor shower and thatched-roof hales (huts) are special treats.

Prince Health Club and Spa

Princeville at Hanalei, 5-4280 Kuhio Hiwy. 800-826-1105. www.princeville.com.

Ocean and garden views greet guests at this full-service spa located in the upscale Princeville at Hanalei resort. Relax in the steam and sauna rooms; take a swim in the five-lane pool and then enjoy one of the Hawaiian-inspired treatments.

Lomilomi massages are popular, as well as the Limu (seaweed) body wrap, and the Hawaiian Salt Glow, guaranteed to leave your sun-dried body baby soft.

Massage in Paradise

"Touching with loving hands" is the literal translation of lomilomi massage. You'll think you've died and gone to heaven when you experience it. The massage technique has been passed down by Hawaiian elders and is now offered in spas throughout the islands. Therapists use both gentle and vigorous kneading strokes and incorporate elbow and forearm work for a deep, all-over body massage. It's firmer and faster than a Swedish massage, leaving you wet-noodle relaxed.

SPAS

OAHU★★★

Aptly nicknamed "The Gathering Place," Oahu ranks as the most bustling and developed of all the islands. Tourists flood the area for its plethora of lodging, dining and shopping venues, and for its waterfront activities. Oahu is also home to the state's most popular tourist attraction, Pearl Harbor's **USS Arizona Memorial★★★**, and to **Iolani Palace★★**, the only royal palace in the US. Visitor information: 877-525-6248 or www.visit-oahu.com.

Most of the island's activity is concentrated in the urban areas of **Honolulu** and **Waikiki**, resting on the south shore. But venture north along Oahu's 125 miles of coastline and you'll find impossibly blue bays, surf-slapped beaches and verdant valleys. Across the Koolau Range from Honolulu extends the lush windward coast of the island, with its suburban communities of Kailua and Kaneohe. West of Pearl Harbor is the drier Waianae coast and the big-wave beaches of Makaha. A route through the agricultural center of Oahu leads to the north shore, fabled for its country living and renowned surfing venues.

Oahu is the second-oldest of the islands. Populated before AD 1000, it was added to the island kingdom in 1795. By 1850, the Hawaiian Royal Court had moved permanently to Honolulu, making it the center of government and commerce for the islands. Today, Oahu, with its 21C vibe and rich, cultural diversity, continues to beat as the heart of Hawaii.

Fast Facts

- At 608 square miles, Oahu is the third-largest of the Hawaiian Islands. The island measures 44 miles long and 30 miles wide at its widest point.
- Three-fourths of Hawaii's population of nearly 1.3 million people live on Oahu.
- Oahu claims the state capital, Honolulu, which also ranks as the state's largest city and the financial center of the Pacific.
- Oahu is the most visited of the Hawaiian Islands.

Aloha Tower Marketplace & Downtown Honolulu Skyline at Sunset

Hawaii Tourism Authority/Chuck Painter

CITIES

From world-class Honolulu to quaint and artsy Haleiwa on the North Shore, Oahu's cities boast rich cultural diversity and must-see sites.

Downtown Honolulu

Brigitta L. House/Michelin

Honolulu★★

Sprawling across the southeast quadrant of Oahu, the world's largest Polynesian city boasts a bustling modern **downtown** of skyscrapers and traffic, extending from Waikiki's surf-washed beaches to the 3,000-foot crest of the jungle-swathed Koolau Range *(from Honolulu Harbor to Vineyard Blvd., between Ward Ave. & River St.)*. Here the first missionaries gathered their Hawaiian congregations and the only royal palace in the US was erected in 1882.

Like most big cities, Honolulu can be congested, noisy, and difficult to get around, so it's best to avoid driving during morning and evening rush hours!

Honolulu Academy of Arts★★ – *900 S. Beretania St., at Ward Ave. See p120.*
Iolani Palace★★ – *S. King & Richard Sts. See p124.*
Kawaiahao Church★ – *957 Punchbowl St. 808-522-1333. www. kawaiahao.org.* King Kamehameha IV married Queen Emma in this venerable house of worship, made from 14,000 blocks of coral cut from the offshore reefs. It took five

Aloha Tower★★

Pier 9, downtown Honolulu. 808-528-5700. www.alohatower.com. Observation deck open year-round daily 9am–5pm. There's no missing this long-time beacon in downtown Honolulu. For nearly eight decades, the ten-story Aloha Tower—named for the greeting etched above its four clock faces (one on each side of the square column)—has greeted cruise-ship passengers and other visitors. Progress may have stripped the 1926 tower's claim to fame as Hawaii's tallest building, but it still offers some of the best views in town from its outdoor observation decks. Bring your credit cards; the **Aloha Tower Marketplace★**, with its shops, galleries and restaurants, surrounds the base of the tower *(see p140)*.

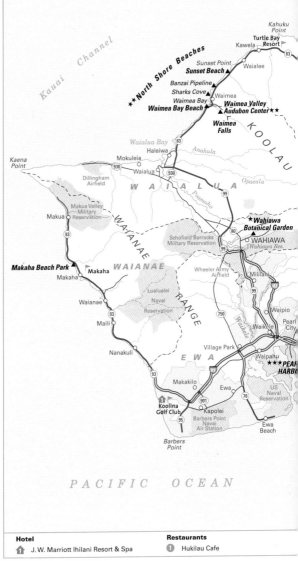

Kahuku Point
Turtle Bay Resort
Kawela
83
★★ North Shore Beaches
Sunset Point
Sunset Beach ▲
Waialee
Waialee
Banzai Pipeline ▲
Sharks Cove ▲
Waimea
Waimea Bay ▲
Waimea Bay Beach ▲
Waimea Valley Audubon Center ★★
Waimea Falls ▲
KOOLAU
Kauai Channel
Waialua Bay
Haleiwa
Mokuleia
83
Anahula
Opaeula
Kaena Point
930
Waialua
930
Peamoho
99
W A I A L U A
Dillingham Airfield
Makua Valley Military Reservation
Makua
93
W A I A N E A
Schofield Barracks Military Reservation
★ Wahiawa Botanical Garden
80
WAHIAWA
Wahiawa Res.
99
Makaha Beach Park
Makaha
Makaha
W A I A N A E
Wheeler Army Airfield
Milani
R A N G E
Waianae
Lualualei Naval Reservation
99
Maili
750
Waikele
Waipio
Pearl City
Waikele
Waikele
Nanakuli
93
E W A
Village Park
Waipahu
★★★ PEARL HARBOR
Makakilo
111
93
Koolina Golf Club
95
901
Kapolei
Barbers Point Naval Air Station
Ewa
US Naval Reservation
76
Ewa Beach
Barbers Point
P A C I F I C   O C E A N

Hotel	**Restaurants**
🏠 J. W. Marriott Ihilani Resort & Spa	❶ Hukilau Cafe

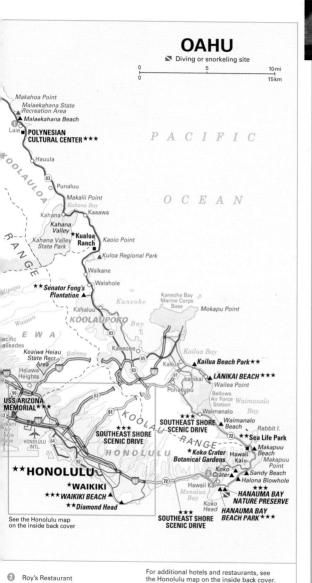

OAHU

◤ Diving or snorkeling site

0 ——— 5 ——— 10 mi
0 ——— 5 ——— 15 km

PACIFIC

OCEAN

Makahoa Point
Malaekahana State
Recreation Area
▲ Malaekahana Beach
Laie
**POLYNESIAN
CULTURAL CENTER ★★★**

○ Hauula

○ Punaluu

Makalii Point
Kahana Bay
Kahana ○ ○ Kaaawa
Kahana
Valley **★Kualoa
Ranch** ▲
Kahana Valley ○ Kaoio Point
State Park
▲ Kuloa Regional Park
○ Waikane
○ Waiahole

**★★Senator Fong's
Plantation** ▲

Kaneohe
Kaneohe Bay
Marine Corps
Base
○ Mokapu Point
○ Kahaluu
KOOLAUPOKO
Bay

○ Kaneohe

Keaiwa Heiau
State Recr.
Area
Halawa Kailua Bay
Heights ○ Kailua **★Kailua Beach Park ★★**
▲ Lanikai **LANIKAI BEACH ★★★**
○ Pohakupu ▲
Wailea Point
Bellows
Air Force
Station Waimanalo
USS ARIZONA Waimanalo Bay
MEMORIAL★★★
▲ Waimanalo
Beach
HONOLULU Rabbit I.
INTL **SOUTHEAST SHORE ★★★**
SCENIC DRIVE **★★Sea Life Park**
Hawaii ★ Makapuu
Kai Beach
★★HONOLULU **★Koko Crater** Makapuu
Botanical Gardens Point
★★★ Koko ▲ Sandy Beach
SOUTHEAST SHORE Crater ▲ Halona Blowhole
SCENIC DRIVE **★★★**
★WAIKIKI Hawaii Kai **HANAUMA BAY**
★★★WAIKIKI BEACH ▲ Manalua **NATURE PRESERVE**
★★Diamond Head Bay **HANAUMA BAY**
Koko **BEACH PARK ★★★**
Head
See the Honolulu map **★★★**
on the inside back cover **SOUTHEAST SHORE**
SCENIC DRIVE

KOOLAULOA

KOOLAU RANGE

EWA

Kipapa

Waiawa

acific
alisades

❷ Roy's Restaurant

For additional hotels and restaurants, see
the Honolulu map on the inside back cover.

years and more than a thousand men to complete the church, which was dedicated in 1842. Today Kawaiahao Church offers Sunday services in Hawaiian and English.

Mission Houses Museum★ –
553 S. King St., at Kawaiahao St. See p122.

Hawaii State Capitol★ –
S. Beretania St., between Richards & Punchbowl Sts. 808-506-0178. Completed in 1969 to replace the capitol at Iolani Palace, this modern structure rises out of a shallow pool to represent volcanoes rising from the sea.

Waikiki★

If you want action, you'll find it here. Once a lounging place for Hawaiian royalty, the suburb of Waikiki is recognized by the forest of towers created by its hotels, its carnival-like atmosphere, and its nonstop activities.

Waikiki Beach, stretching 1.5 miles from Ala Wai Canal to Diamond Head, remains one of the best

Statue of Duke Paoa Kahanamoku, Waikiki Beach

Brigitta L. House/Michelin

places in the world to learn surfing, a sport invented here hundreds of years ago. At Waikiki Beach Center stands a statue of Duke Kahanamoku *(Kalakaua Ave. near Kaiulani Ave.)*, Hawaii's three-time Olympic swimming champion (1912–1920), who introduced surfing to California and Australia. Non-surfers may ride the waves in an outrigger canoe or take a cruise on a sailboat that casts off right from the shoreline.

Kapiolani Park – Located at the east end of Waikiki, 140-acre Kapiolani Park encompasses the **Honolulu Zoo** *(see p135)* and **Waikiki Shell**, a venue for open-air concerts and the late-morning *Kodak Hula Show*.

International Market Place★

Opposite Waikiki Beach, this outdoor marketplace, set around the same giant banyan tree for half a century, is a great place for cheap souvenirs. It's chock-full of pick-a-pearl stands, shell necklaces, T-shirts, beach mats, towels and sarongs.
2330 Kalakaua Ave., next to Waikiki Town Center. 808-971-2080. www.internationalmarketplace waikiki.com. Open year-round daily 10am–10:30pm.

Waikiki Beach

Brigitta L. House/Michelin

MUST SEE OAHU

BEACHES

Waikiki, Waimea and Lanikai beaches are well-known hot spots, but you'll also find secluded gems along the island's 112 miles of coastline.

> **Touring Tip**
> A residential neighborhood development sits in front of Lanikai Beach, but you'll find several beach-access walkways off Mokulua Drive. Snag an on-street parking spot where you can.

Lanikai Beach★★★

In Lanikai, on the east shore. Access via public walkways off Mokulua Dr.

It's no wonder this sun-drenched oasis on Oahu's east shore is a magnet for photographers—and ranks as one of the top beaches in the US. Picture paradise: a white, sandy beach fringed with palm trees and fragrant tropical plants, licked by crystal-clear, aqua-blue surf. That's Lanikai Beach. This nearly mile-long jewel has the added bonus of calm waters, making it perfect for swimming, too. If you're feeling energetic, you can kayak to the nearby islands of Mokumanu and Mokulua. Bring your binoculars; both islands are great for bird-watching. For a special treat, arrive at Lanikai at dawn for the best view of the rising sun you're likely to see anywhere.

Waikiki Beach★★★

On Oahu's south shore, from the Outrigger Canoe Club at 2909 Kalakaua Ave. to Kahanamoku Lagoon at 2005 Kalia Rd.

This 1.5-mile stretch of sand, flanked by high-rise hotels and warm, turquoise waters, is one of the best big-city beaches in the world. It's also one of the most famous, drawing more than four million visitors a year to its high-energy, people-packed shoreline. Running from the dramatic Diamond Head crater to the Ala Wai Yacht Harbor, the beach was once swampland, referred to by ancient Hawaiians as *Waikiki*, or "spouting water." Today it's a hotbed of activity; if you like to be in the center of

Lanikai Beach

Brigitta L. House/Michelin

Waikiki Beach with Diamond Head in the background

Brigitta L. House/Michelin

the action, this is it. Waikiki Beach offers something for everyone: gentle waters for bathers; big, offshore breaks for surfers; and 80-degree waters for swimming. You can snag a warm patch of soft sand, slather yourself with lotion, and spend the day relaxing in the sun. Or pick your pleasure: rent an outrigger canoe, take a surfing lesson (a variety of on-the-beach outfitters offer instruction for all ages), snorkel, play beach volleyball… the list is nearly endless. Stop for a brain-freezing but delicious shave ice on busy **Kalakaua Avenue**,

---

Touring Tip

Waikiki is actually a series of connecting beaches; each has its own name and each has something special to offer. For fabulous sunset viewing, head to the beach in front of the Outrigger Reef on the Beach. For sea-turtle watching, look offshore near the breakwater in front of the Moana Surfrider. Families will appreciate the calm waters in front of the Royal Hawaiian Hotel. For picnics, consider lovely Kapiolani Park *(see p108)* at the foot of Diamond Head.

---

and take in the sights, sounds and smells of this infamous outdoor playground—it's sensory overload, for sure!

Kailua Beach Park★★

East shore, at the end of Kailua Rd.

You'll find this beachy gem on the windward side of the island, just around the corner from Lanikai Beach *(see p109)*. Wide, sloping sands and safe, calm waters make this a perfect place for sunbathing and swimming. There's also good parking, concessions, lifeguards, picnic areas, restrooms and showers on-site, adding to the overall comfort level. Kailua's fine, soft sand stretches for a mile, and the swaying palms and offshore islands in the distance make a postcard-pretty backdrop.

While the setting is serene, there's likely to be a lot of action on the water. Kailua Beach is a world-class windsurfing locale, drawing some of the best in the sport.

Pull up your beach chair and take a front-row seat. Or get in on the action yourself; shops in the nearby town of Kailua offer gear and lessons.

Giovanni's Shrimp

Beach boys, wave riders, hungry locals and savvy visitors know fresh shrimp (and a good deal!) when they taste it. That's why Giovanni's Shrimp is the favorite nosh on the north shore. You'll find this battered lunch truck parked along Highway 83, between Turtle Bay and Kahuku. Order up a heaping, half-pound plate of farm-raised, steamed Kauai shrimp, then top it with garlic or hot chili sauce. It doesn't get much better than this!

North Shore Beaches★★

During the winter months, the seven-mile string of beaches ringing Oahu's northern waters is most famous for its hugely popular surfing venues. **Sunset Beach Park** is a lovely stretch of white sand and clear waters—though often calm in the summer, there's raging surf in the winter. The point is a good spot for tidepooling. **Waimea Bay Beach Park** is said to have the wildest, most dangerous surf in the world. Spectators line the beach during the winter months when the surf can reach 30 feet or more. **Ehukai Beach Park**, is best known for the **Banzai Pipeline**, a legendary tubed surfing break.
Note: When visiting any of the North Shore beaches, remember to read the posted warnings, ask lifeguards about swimming conditions, and adhere to Oahu's common sense law: If in doubt, stay out!

Sharks! – If you're very lucky you may be able to spot the fins of white-tipped reef sharks at **Sharks Cove**, on Oahu's north shore. But for guaranteed shark spotting, **Hawaii Shark Encounters** (*808-351-9373; www.hawaiishark encounters.com; departures are weather dependent; $112 adults, under 12 years $75; no under 5s*) offers shark encounters from the safety of a plexi-glass cage. It's not uncommon to have 30 sharks circling around and nudging the cage!

🐢 "From Here to Eternity" Beach

Located below the Halona Blowhole parking lot.

Put on your best walking shoes and climb down the steep hill to this secluded beach, protected by the surrounding sea cliffs and crags. Most people are turned off by the trek down and back up, but you'll be glad you didn't wimp out! A long, sloping sandy bottom calms the open-ocean surf, making it a good place for swimming for much of the year.
Look for sea turtles that hang out in the cove.

Giant wave at Waimea Bay, North Shore

Hawaii Tourism Authority/Kirk Lee Aeder

BEACHES

Life's a Beach

Hawaii's beaches are gloriously open to the public, and that includes hotel beaches. Of course, you'll pay for using cabanas and ordering fruity beverages! At most hotel beaches, you'll find lifeguards and loads of facilities; at public beach parks, facilities vary, but restrooms can be unsavory. Don't count on lifeguards, either, but look for warning signs and flags to indicate unsafe swimming conditions: a yellow flag means there's a lifeguard on duty; blue means it's dangerous to swim; red means no swimming allowed. You probably won't pay an entrance fee, nor will you pay for parking.

Yokohama Bay Beach

Take H-1 West until it connects to Farrington Hwy. The beach is located at the end of Farrington Hwy.

This is the perfect place to spend a day. Pack a picnic basket, plenty of bottled water—and a fishing pole if you like to dangle a line. This hidden beach on the Waianae coast is rarely crowded, and the waters calm during the summer months. The surf during the winter months, however, can be treacherous but a lure for local surfers who tackle the 20-foot waves. It's a great place for shell collecting and snorkeling, too.

Stick around for some amazing sunset viewing.

PARKS AND NATURAL SITES

Explore volcanic tuff cones and craters, underwater preserves, ancient ruins and sacred waterfalls.

Diamond Head★★

Diamond Head Rd., Waikiki Beach. Open year-round daily 6am–6pm.

You can't miss it: this 760-foot-high natural landmark is a dominating feature in Oahu. The volcanic tuff cone and crater, once the site of an ancient Hawaiian temple, has been extinct for more than 150,000 years. Legend has it that ancient Hawaiian kings worshipped at

View of Diamond Head from Kapiolani Park

Hawaii Tourism Authority/ Tor Johnson

the site and that some of the last human sacrifices were performed here.

In the 1800s, British sailors named the crater Diamond Head when they mistook calcite crystals for diamonds shining in the lava rock. Remnants of Fort Ruger, built on the crater in the early 1900s, can still be seen.

● **Best reason to visit Diamond Head:** To walk the trail to the summit for incredible views— some of the best on Oahu.

Hanauma Bay Nature Preserve★★★

Off Hwy. 72 in Hanauma Bay (10mi east of Waikiki). 808-396-4229. www.honolulu.gov/parks/ facility/hanaumabay/welcome. htm. Open Jun–Aug Wed–Mon 6am–7pm (second and fourth Sat of the month until 10pm). Rest of the year Wed–Mon 6am–6pm. $5 (free for children ages 12 & under).

This stunningly beautiful horse-shoe-shape reef, surrounded by coral sand and the sunken walls of an ancient volcano, is one of America's top beaches and one of the most popular in all Hawaii. Up to 3,000 people visit Hanauma Bay each day to swim in its warm

Hiking Diamond Head
Pack your sunscreen, sturdy boots and plenty of bottled water before heading to the base of Diamond Head for the short hike to the summit. The hike is a round-trip of less than two miles, but includes some steep sections, and more than 270 steps! It's worth every grunt and groan: you'll be rewarded with sweeping views of Oahu's stunning southeast coastline.

emerald-green waters and snorkel among schools of brilliantly colored tropical fish.

Technically, the reef is now designated a State Underwater Park and Conservation District and strict conservation efforts in recent years have begun to pay off. Feeding fish is now banned at the preserve, and all visitors must watch a mandatory conservation and safety video.

Tip: The park limits the number of guests; arrive early in the morning because once the parking lot is full, you'll be turned away.

Snorkeling – The reef is perfect for snorkeling year-round (masks, fins and snorkels are available for rent at the visitor center). Here, more than 150 species of fish might flitter around your fins.

Under the Sea
Don't you dare leave the islands without donning a mask and flippers and peering into the deep! Hawaii's reefs are generally smaller and younger than others in the Pacific, but alive and colorful nonetheless. There are about 680 species of fish in the islands and 40 species of reef-building corals. You're likely to see cauliflower coral, lobe coral and finger coral. Look for urchins, sea cucumbers, snails, damselfish, triggerfish, puffers, yellow tangs, snappers and spotted eagle rays. You may also spot some, like the Hawaiian cleaner wrasse and the pebbled and millseed butterfly fish, which are only found in Hawaii.

PARKS AND NATURAL SITES

SCENIC DRIVES

Flip the car top down and take off through vibrant neighborhoods, lush valleys, and along the 112-mile coastline. *See map pp106–107.*

Halona Blowhole

Brigitta L. House/Michelin

Southeast Shore★★★

Begin at the town of Waikiki and go east on the H-1 Freeway to Hwy. 72.

This 30-mile loop drive along Oahu's southeast shore features the island's most spectacular scenery

and some of its more popular sites. You can do this drive in a half-day, but better to take your time and plan a day for the trip.

It will be crowded, typically packed with tour buses and slow-driving visitors—all the more reason to take your time.

There are plenty of great stops for swimming and sightseeing along the way.

Head out of Waikiki on H-1 to Highway 72, and follow it east as it curves around the rugged coastline. Your first stop is pretty **Hanauma Bay★★★** *(see p113).* This protected Marine Reserve features some of the island's best snorkeling.

As you leave the bay and circle around the Koko Head area, the coastline becomes much more rugged, and you'll have fine views of waves crashing against rocky outcrops. About 2 miles past the bay is the turn-off for the **Halona Blowhole**, where the water gushes and spouts through under-

Aerial view of Hanauma Bay

Hawaii Tourism Authority/Heather Titus

Hawaii Tourism Authority/Chuck Painter

View from Pali Lookout

water lava tubes and tunnels.
A short distance to the northeast
you'll find **Sandy Beach**, popular
with boogie boarders, bodysurf-
ers and kite-flyers *(see box, p136)*.
Across the road is **Koko Crater**.
Inside the crater are the **Koko
Crater Botanical Gardens★**
(see p117), a nice place to stretch
your legs and take in top-of-the-
crater views. As Highway 72 winds
around Makapuu Point, up the
east coast of Oahu, sweeping vistas open up to the sea and Koolau
Range that hugs the coastline.
Ready to get out of the car again?
Take the short half-hour trail to the
summit of Makapuu Point with

views of Rabbit Island and beautiful **Makapuu Beach** *(trailhead is
1.5mi north of Sandy Beach; park
and walk along the service road to
the lighthouse)*.
Continue north and you'll pass
Sea Life Park★★ *(see p134)* and
Waimanalo Beach, a good place
to stop for a swim.
Take the coastal route and you'll
end up in the bustling town of
Kailua. From here, take Pali Road
(Route 61), back to Honolulu,
leading across the jagged Koolau
Range. A final must-stop along the
way is the scenic **Pali Lookout**,
with awesome mountain views.

Through the Rain Forest

If you're looking for a short drive that feels worlds away from the hustle and
bustle of Honolulu, take scenic **Tantalus Drive**. The two-hour excursion, minutes
from downtown, takes you through a tropical preserve and the rolling foothills
of the Koolau Range. *Take the Wilder St. exit off H-1 and follow Wilder to Makiki St.
Turn right on Makiki St. and then left on Round Top Dr.; Round Top becomes Tantalus
Dr. Continue around to Makiki Heights Rd., and loop back to Makiki St.*
You'll climb to about 2,000 feet and have expansive views of downtown Honolulu, Diamond Head, Waikiki and Pearl Harbor. Hikes, through rain forests and
thick bamboo stands off Tantalus Drive, range from one hour to a full day.
For trail information, call the Division of Forestry and Wildlife: 808-587-0166.

SCENIC DRIVES

GARDENS

Oahu's botanical gardens and nature preserves—some of the finest in the country— boast an impressive array of exotic and rare plants.

Foster
Botanical
Garden

Brigitta L. House/Michelin

Foster Botanical Garden★

180 N. Vineyard Blvd., Honolulu. 808-522-7060. www.honolulu. gov/parks/hbg/fbg.htm. Open year-round daily 9am–4pm. Closed Jan 1 & Dec 25. $5.

Garden enthusiasts won't want to miss this 14-acre botanical gem on the north side of Honolulu's

A-Mazing

Dole Plantation *(808-621-8408; www. dole-plantation.com)* boasts the largest maze in the world. The two-acre maze includes 1.7 miles of paths and more than 11,000 plants. Stop and smell the hibiscus as you contemplate your next turn!

Chinatown, a flowery, exotic oasis smack-dab in the middle of the city! And where else can you see the nearly extinct wild East African Gigasipha macrosiphon, with its evening-opening white flowers? Or the rare native Hawaiian loulu palm? Or, how about a double coconut palm that can drop 50-pound nuts? There are plenty of unusual and rare specimens here, all neatly organized according to plant groups. The more than 150-year-old garden began when German botanist and physician William Hillebrand leased a tract of land from Queen Kalama. Some of the original trees Hillebrand planted are still standing.

Let Me Lei it on You!

You'll find some of the best displays of leis at the stands in **Chinatown**. Familiar favorites are still made with plumeria, ginger, orchid, ilima and carnation flowers, but you'll see more permanent varieties, too, made with nuts, herbs, seashells and dried leaves.

Hawaii Tourism Authority/ Tor Johnson

The ancient Hawaiians presented leis to their gods during religious ceremonies to insure their blessings. Today, as in the past, leis are given and worn to mark memorable moments in life, special occasions and celebrations. Want to string your own necklace of flowers? Complimentary lei-making lessons are offered at many hotels and resorts throughout Hawaii.

Koko Crater Botanical Gardens

Brigitta L. House/Michelin

🌿 Koko Crater Botanical Gardens

Off Kealahou St. from Hwy. 72, on Koko Head. 808-522-7060. www.co.honolulu.hi.us/parks/ hbg/kcbg.htm. Open year-round daily sunrise to sunset. Closed Jan 1 & Dec 25. 90min self-guided tour. Free.

Best part about this place? Even if you're not a gardening aficionado, you'll appreciate the dramatic crater setting. Koko Crater is a volcanic tuff cone, created some 10,000 years ago. The 60-acre basin is home to a newly developing, hot and dry garden of desert-loving plants. Take the 2-mile self-guided walk through the garden, then head over to nearby Sandy Beach to cool off.

Lyon Arboretum★

3860 Manoa Rd., Honolulu. 808-988-0456. www.hawaii.edu/ lyonarboretum/index.php. Open year-round Mon–Fri 9am–4pm, Sat 9am–3pm. Closed major holidays. $5.

This 193-acre nature preserve showcases more than 5,000 exotic trees and plants found in Hawaii. The woodsy oasis is crisscrossed with walking paths through stands of mountain apple, candlenut trees and taro, and along grand

©Daderot/Wikimedia Commons

Lyon Arboretum

GARDENS

Touring Tip

Why not make a day of it? Stop at Wahiawa Botanical Garden on your way to the north shore, where you can take in the surfing scene at **Waimea Bay**, and take the kids to **Waimea Valley★★** *(see p130).*

patches of ferns, bromeliads and magnolias. Take the trail up to Inspiration Point for pretty valley views; along the way, stop at the bo tree, a descendant of the tree that Gautama Buddha sat under for enlightenment. Just beyond the arboretum, you'll find the hiking trail to 100-foot **Manoa Falls**.

Senator Fong's Plantation★★

47-285 Pulama Rd., off Hwy. 83, Kaneohe. 808-239-6775. www.fonggarden.net. Open year-round daily 10am–2pm. Closed Jan 1 & Dec 25. $14.50.

An open-air tram ride takes you through these gardens, featuring over 70 edible varieties of fruits and nuts, 80 different types of palms, slopes of pili grass (once used to make thatch houses), a collection of early Polynesian plants, and 100 rare sandalwood trees. An easy one-mile guided walking tour is also offered. The gardens embrace 725 acres, rising from 80 feet to 2,600 feet above sea level. Owned by Hiram L. Fong, the first Asian American elected to the US Senate, the plan-

tation is divided into five areas, each named after presidents Fong served with during his 17 years in the US Senate.

When you're not taking in the sights and scents of the flora, take a peek at the Koolau Range and the vast ocean views.

Wahiawa Botanical Garden★

1396 California Ave., Wahiawa. 802-421-7321. www.honolulu. gov/parks/hbg/wbg.htm. Open year-round daily 9am–4pm. Closed Jan 1 & Dec 25.

Take a deep breath, stop, and smell the… spices! This 27-acre rain-forest garden overflows with West Indies spice trees (allspice, nutmeg, ginger), palms and pom poms—all tropical plants that require a cool, moist environment.

Pick up a map *(free)* at the information desk, then walk the terraced paths down into a shady, humid ravine. Bring your raincoat—the area gets 52 to 80 inches of rainfall each year.

Tree Ferns – The garden has a large collection of tree ferns, both the Hawaiian variety and tree ferns from other tropical places, such as Australia and Tasmania. The seeds of large, leafy Hawaiian tree ferns *(Cibotium glaucum)* most likely came to the islands on the wind, millions of years ago. These ancient plants still form the understory of many of the state's forests.

Red, White, and Pink

More than 5,000 varieties of hibiscus grow in Hawaii, including a number of natives, like the hau tree with flowers that change from yellow to orange, and the sweet-smelling kokio keokeo, which can reach heights of up to 60 feet.

OAHU

MUST SEE

MUSEUMS

Had enough fun in the sun? No problem; cosmopolitan Oahu has top-notch art, cultural, and history museums.

Bishop Museum and Planetarium

Bishop Museum and Planetarium★★★

1525 Bernice St., Honolulu. 808-847-3511. www.bishopmus eum.org. Open year-round daily 9am–5pm. Closed Dec 25. $15.95 adults, $12.95 children (ages 4–12).

If you only have time to see one museum on Oahu, make it this one. Considered one of Hawaii's finest museums, the sprawling Museum of Natural and Cultural History is the state's largest; its collection of Hawaiian and Pacific artifacts is regarded as one of the best in the world, including more than 187,000 artifacts, documents and photographs relating to Hawaii and other Pacific island cultures.

What's What at the Bishop?

Hawaiian Hall★★★ – The three-story Victorian-style gallery houses objects of Hawaiian culture from the Stone Age to the 21C. You can't miss the 55-foot sperm whale

Beyond the Exhibits: Guided Tours at Bishop Museum

For a great introduction to the Bishop Museum, catch one of the free, 15- or 20-minute guided tours, offered in Hawaiian Hall. Several tours and demonstrations are scheduled throughout the day. Are you interested in native plants and traditional gardening? Show up for the 25-minute tour of the museum's gardens. In addition, live music and dance performances and storytelling sessions are held daily and free lei-making and hula lessons are offered at the museum's Learning Activity area.

Polynesian Hall, Bishop Museum and Planetarium

OAHU

suspended from the ceiling
(a tribute to Hawaii's whaling past)
or the magnificent ceremonial
robes made from the feathers of
thousands of birds.

Polynesian Hall★★ – Two floors
are chock-full of artifacts from
Pacific cultures across Polynesia,
Micronesia and Melanesia.

Natural History Hall★ – Housed
in the Castle Building in the
modern wing of the museum, this
gallery is a favorite among families.
You'll get an up-close look at some
of Hawaii's rare, endemic birds
and insects. Kids will appreciate
the hands-on activities geared
specially toward them.

Feather cape of King Kamehameha

Hawaii Tourism Japan

120

Kahili Room★ -- This small gallery
displays an impressive collection
of kahili, the feather staffs traditionally used at royal ceremonies.

**Jhamandas Watumull
Planetarium★** – What's different
about the sky over Hawaii? Find
out for yourself in a series of changing shows, included in the museum admission *(daily at 11:30am,
12:45pm, 1:30pm & 3:30pm).*

Honolulu Academy of Arts★

*900 S. Beretania St., Honolulu. 808-
532-8701. www.honoluluacademy.
org. Open year-round Tue–Sat
10am–4:30pm, Sun 1pm–5pm.
Closed major holidays. $10 adults
(free for children ages 12 and
under).*

This world-class museum features
more than 34,000 pieces of art and
is internationally recognized for its
extensive Asian collection—
considered one of the finest in the
country. Housed in an award-
winning Mediterranean-style
building, the collections are
equally divided between Western
and Asian art. More than 30
galleries surround six landscaped
courtyards, including the Henry
R. Luce Pavilion, home to the
museum's permanent collection of
traditional Hawaiian art.

Asian Art★★ – The collection
consists of more than 16,000
objects from China, Japan, Korea
and Southeast Asia. You'll see
some 300 Japanese paintings
from the 12C to the 20C. Also of
note: Buddhist cave sculpture
dating from the 4C to the 10C;
the collection of *Scenes of Kyoto*,
painted by well-known Japanese
artist Kano Motohide; and author

Honolulu Academy of Art

Under the Monkey Pod Tree

Bet you worked up an appetite roaming the more than 30 galleries of the Honolulu Academy of Arts. No problem. Head to the **Pavilion Café**, popular with locals, and non-museum visitors, too. The open-air eatery serves up fresh-made island dishes (like the mahi and soba noodle salad) against a backdrop of ferns and palms, swirling fans and teak furniture. Tables overlook gardens, waterfalls, and glass sculptures by Jun Kaneko. Pull up a seat under the shade of the 70-year-old monkey pod tree. *The café is open Tue–Sat 11:30am–1:30pm; call 808-532-8734 for reservations.*

James Michener's collection of woodblock prints.

Western Art★★ – There are more than 15,000 works from European and US artists here, including paintings, sculptures, crafts, furniture, textiles and graphic works. Paintings by Paul Cézanne, Vincent Van Gogh, Claude Monet, Henri Matisse and others can be found in the European gallery.

Hawaiian Art★ – This gallery displays indigenous and traditional Hawaiian art and artifacts, from 18C works to contemporary sculpture, paintings and photographs.

Shangri La★

Tours depart from the Honolulu Academy of Arts, 900 S. Beretania St., Honolulu. 866-385-3859. www.shangrilahawaii.org. Visit by 2½-hour guided tour only, Nov–Aug Wed–Sat 8:30am–1:30pm. Closed Jan 1, Jul 4, Thanksgiving Day & Dec 25. $25.

Imagine an Islamic palace in Hawaii and you have Shangri La, the private estate of Doris Duke, the wealthy, only child of American tobacco baron James Duke. Built in 1937, Shangri La features Duke's eclectic collection of Islamic art,

©David Franzen/Doris Duke Foundation for Islamic Art

Shangri La

which she amassed over a span of almost 60 years. More than 3,500 objects are displayed throughout the home's exterior and interior spaces, which are exquisitely decorated with painted and gilded wood ceilings, intricate mosaic panels and bright textiles.

Mission Houses Museum★★

553 S. King St., at Kawaiahao St., Honolulu. 808-531-0481. www.missionhouses.org. Open year-round Tue–Sat 10am–4pm. Closed major holidays. $10.

The pieces of Hawaii's oldest Western-style structure were shipped around Cape Horn from New England and assembled here in 1821 by the first American Calvinist missionaries, with the help of the Hawaiian people. With the coming of the missionaries, Hawaii's culture changed forever. You'll learn how by taking a self-guided or guided tour of these three historic houses, which date from 1821 to 1841.

Polynesian Cultural Center★★★

55–370 Kamehameha Hwy. (Rte. 83), Laie. 808-293-3333 or 800-367-7060. www.polynesia. com. Open year-round Mon–Sat 11am–6:30pm. Closed Thanksgiving Day & Dec 25. $58 adults for general admission and evening show, $47 children (ages 3–11).

This cultural theme park is Hawaii's number-one paid attraction. Located on the north shore of Oahu, about 25 miles from downtown Honolulu, the Polynesian Cultural Center features the islands

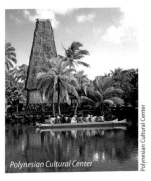

Polynesian Cultural Center

of Hawaii, Samoa, Aotearoa (Maori, New Zealand), Fiji, the Marquesas, Tahiti and Tonga, spread out across a 42-acre setting. You could spend all afternoon here, wandering the villages, touring island dwellings and learning about traditional skills. Hands-on activities and demonstrations are held throughout the day. For example, on Hawaii,

Polynesian Cultural Center

you can discover the heritage of the hula, practice lei-making, and see how taro is harvested and cooked into poi. On the Marquesas, you can get a temporary tattoo featuring traditional artwork. On Tonga, there are drumming presentations, or try your hand at *tolo* (spear throwing).
The Center recently opened the Halau Waa, or canoe house of learning. The $2.65 million facility

houses a losepa voyaging canoe; exhibits showcase Polynesian voyaging techniques.

The Contemporary Museum

2411 Makiki Heights Dr., Honolulu. 808-526-1322. www.tcmhi.org. Open year-round Tue–Sat 10am–4pm, Sun noon–4pm. Closed major holidays. $5 adults (free for children ages 12 and under).

Set on 3.5 acres of sculpture and meditation gardens, the small museum displays changing exhibitions of modern art pieces by leading and emerging contemporary artists. It's worthwhile taking one of the docent-led tours conducted at 1:30pm each afternoon, which offer information on the works presented throughout the five galleries.

Hawaii Maritime Center

Pier 7, downtown Honolulu. 808-536-6373. www.bishop museum.org/exhibits/hmc/hmc. html. Open year-round daily 9am–5pm. Closed Dec 25. $8.50 adults, $5.50 children (ages 6–17).

This is one of the top places in the islands to learn about Hawaii's colorful seafaring past; it's both entertaining and informative for the entire family. Kids especially enjoy the humpback whale skeleton and the on-going videos of surfing champions, including old-time surfing great, Duke Kahanamoku. There's also an impressive 1,805-pound blue marlin, caught off the coast of Makaha. Grab a walkman and a cassette for an audio tour of the King Kalakaua Boathouse, where you'll learn of pirates and kings, shipwrecks and sharks. The waterfront center, located near the Aloha Tower (see p105), is home to the world's only four-masted, fully rigged ship (walk the decks!) and a 60-foot double-hulled sailing canoe.

Hawaii Maritime Center

Hawaii Maritime Center

MUSEUMS

HISTORIC SITES

The top tourist attraction in the state (Pearl Harbor) and the only royal palace in the country are highlights of Oahu's must-see sites.

Iolani Palace

Brigitta L. House/Michelin

Iolani Palace★★

S. King & Richards Sts., Honolulu. 808-522-0822. www.iolanipalace. org. Open year-round Tue–Sat 9am–5pm. Self-guided gallery tours $6; guided grand tours $20.

This rococo structure, a dominant feature in downtown Honolulu, is the only royal palace in the United States. If you're intrigued with kings and queens, join the 90-minute docent-led tour of three floors of the four-story palace, with plenty of history provided. You can also roam the galleries on your own for a peek at rare treasures and crown jewels, including the king's crown, studded with 521 diamonds, 54 pearls, 20 opals, eight emeralds, eight rubies, and other jewels, as well as a temple drum carved from a coconut tree and decorated with human teeth. King David Kalakaua, back from

travels in Europe, erected the palace in 1882; its last royal occupant was Queen Lili'uokalani, whose government was overthrown in 1893. Across King Street stands a statue of **Kamehameha the Great**. A modern statue of Lili'uokalani graces the other side of the palace facing the capitol.

Palace Highlights

Throne Room – Dripping with crimson and gold, the Throne Room hosted many a royal ball and reception over the years. It also served as a meeting place for the House of Representatives from 1893 to 1968, when the Palace served as the Territorial and, later, the State capitol.

Statue of Lili'uokalani

Brigitta L. House/Michelin

State Dining Room – With its ornate, carved sliding doors and three massive sideboards, the dining room was used for State dinners. The Senate Chamber was housed in this room before the new state capitol was completed in 1969.

Coronation Pavilion – Built in 1883 for the coronation of King Kalakaua and Queen Kapiolani, the pavilion stands in the corner of the grounds *(near King & Richards Sts.)*. In more recent times, several of Hawaii's governors were inaugurated here.

Pearl Harbor★★★

6mi west of downtown Honolulu via H-1 Freeway & Kamehameha Hwy. (Rte. 90).

The infamous bay, site of the attack that hurled the United States into World War II, is Hawaii's most popular tourist attraction, drawing nearly 1.5 million visitors each year. A visit will surely stir your patriotic blood. Here on December 7, 1941, more than 2,300 servicemen were killed in a surprise early-morning Japanese air attack on the US naval fleet anchored in the bay. Eighteen ships, including six battleships and three destroyers, sank in America's

---

Queen Emma Summer Palace

2913 Pali Hwy. 808-595-6291. www.daughtersofhawaii.com/ summerpalace. $6.

For a peek at royal life, visit the palace where Emma, wife of King Kamehameha IV, spent her summers. Emma was of Hawaiian-British heritage and thus was an early symbol of cosmopolitanism in the isles. Royal Hawaiian and personal artifacts are displayed in her Victorian-era Nuuanu Valley retreat.

---

greatest military disaster. President Franklin Roosevelt declared it "a date which will live in infamy" as America plunged into World War II. The harbor is still surrounded by active military bases, but it also includes three must-see visitor sites.

USS Arizona Memorial★★★

1 Arizona Memorial Dr., Honolulu. 808-422-0561. www.nps.gov/usar. Open year-round daily 7:30am– 5:30pm. Boat trips 7:45am–3pm. Closed Jan 1, Thanksgiving Day & Dec 25.

Perhaps no war memorial is more poignant than the *USS Arizona*. Floating over the hulk of the

---

Visiting the USS Arizona Memorial

No matter what time of year you go, you'll run into mobs of tourists. Boat-launch tickets can run out by noon, and waits at the launch can be as long as two hours. The tickets are given on a first-come, first-served basis and each individual must pick up his/ her own ticket. Your best bet: Show up when the visitor center opens at 7:30am (lines begin as early as 6am) to pick up boat-launch tickets, then browse the exhibits and museum gift shop while you wait for the launch.

Waikiki's Historic Resort Tours

Join the popular (free) tour of the historic, more than 100-year-old Moana Surfrider, A Westin Resort & Spa, offered at 11am and 5pm every Mon, Wed, and Fri *(2365 Kalakaua Ave., Honolulu; see p185)*. Along with a peek at this turn-of-the-century icon—Waikiki's first beach resort—you'll hear funny insider tales of life on Oahu. Also, check out the hotel's second-floor museum with old-time photographs of former guests.

sunken battleship, the concave, 184-foot white-concrete bridge marks the permanent tomb of 1,177 sailors killed in the Pearl Harbor attack. Each victim's name is inscribed in white marble on one wall. The macabre outline of the ship's hull is visible below. Launches depart on a first-come, first-served basis from a shoreline visitor center, where historical exhibits and a 25-minute documentary film are presented. This is a very popular site; be prepared to wait in line an hour or more.

USS Arizona Memorial

USS Bowfin Submarine Museum & Park★

11 Arizona Memorial Dr., Honolulu. 808-423-1341. www.bowfin.org. Open year-round daily 8am–5pm (last tour of submarine at 4:30pm). Closed Jan 1, Thanksgiving Day & Dec 25. Submarine & museum tour $10 adults, $4 children (ages 4–12). Museum only $5 adults, $3 children. Children under age 4 are not permitted on the submarine, but may visit the museum and mini-theater at no charge. Tickets and trolley shuttles to the Battleship Missouri Memorial (see p127) are available here.

A walk through the *Bowfin*, credited with sinking 44 Japanese ships, helps define the claustrophobia of submarine missions. Visitors are given cassette players narrating their tour through the cramped spaces. The additional 10,000-square-foot on-site museum showcases submarine life with a

Touring Tip

History doesn't have to be boring! Have your kids pick up a free Junior Ranger booklet at the front desk of the *USS Arizona* Memorial Visitor Center. The fun-filled book, best for ages 7 to 12, guides kids through the events of the infamous attack on Pearl Harbor, with colorful photos, sketches and activities. Added bonus: They get a Junior Ranger badge when they complete the book.

collection of artifacts, weapons, missiles and memorabilia.

Waterfront Memorial – Honors the 52 American submarines and the more than 3,500 submariners lost during World War II.

Battleship Missouri Memorial★

11 Arizona Memorial Dr., Honolulu. Access only by shuttle bus from the USS Bowfin Submarine Museum and Park; tickets and trolley shuttles are available there. 808-455-1600 or 877-MIGHTYMO. www.ussmissouri.com. Open year-round daily 9am–5pm (ticket window closes at 4pm). Closed Jan 1, Thanksgiving Day & Dec 25. Museum only $16 adults, $8 children. A variety of guided tours are also offered.

USS Missouri Memorial Association

USS Missouri

This historic battleship, docked near the remains of the *USS Arizona*, features the site of the September 2, 1945 surrender that ended World War II.

The six-deck ship is chock-full of models, maps, photographs and other exhibits.

You can meander through the rooms, including the gunfire-control station, mess deck, galley, bakery, ship's store and sleeping

area, and browse the exhibits.

Tip: You'll get more out of the visit if you **sign up for the one-hour guided tour**. Tour guests also get to experience a flight simulation of the assault on Iwo Jima in 1943 aboard a plane that was launched from the deck of the *Missouri*.

National Memorial Cemetery of the Pacific★

2177 Puowaina Dr., Honolulu. 808-532-3720. www.cem.va.gov/CEMs/nchp/nmcp.asp. Open Mar–Sept daily 8am–6:30pm; Oct–Mar daily 8am–5:30pm; Memorial Day 7am–7pm.

Occupying an extinct crater known simply as The Punchbowl, the "Arlington of the Pacific" (a reference to Arlington National Cemetery in Virginia) is the final resting place for the more than 40,000 US military men and others whom the government has honored.

Many come to visit the graves of World War II correspondent, Ernie Pyle, and Hawaii's astronaut, Ellison Onizuka, who died in the Challenger space-shuttle disaster of 1986.

The Punchbowl – The crater in which the cemetery rests was formed between 75,000 and 100,000 years ago. Ironically, the site's Hawaiian name, Puowaina, translates to "Hill of Sacrifice"; ancient islanders once offered human sacrifices to the gods here. During the reign of Kamehameha the Great, cannons were mounted at the rim of the crater to salute distinguished arrivals.

Later, it was used as a rifle range for the Hawaii National Guard before the national cemetery was approved in 1948.

FOR FUN

Not surprisingly, entertainment centers around outdoor recreation, like snorkeling, surfing and sunset cruises.

Surfing as a Spectator Sport★★★

Surf's up! No trip to Oahu would be complete without watching the rip-roaring antics and athleticism of the island's top surfers. Oahu is touted as the surfing capital of the world, renowned for its big-water beaches, high-profile championships, and famous surfing personalities. The waters off Oahu feature 600 different types of surf breaks, offering gentle breaks for beginners and formidable surf for the most experienced wave riders. For the best shows, head to Oahu's north shore.

Sunset Beach – *North of Waimea, on the north shore.* Here you'll find a pretty two-mile band of sand and some of the best surfers in the world. Throw your blanket down, take a seat, and watch the show. You're likely to see talented surfers riding powerful, 15-foot and

Sun, Surf and Snow Cones

All that sun and surf pique your thirst? While you're on the north shore, head to **Matsumoto's** *(66–087 Kamehameha Hwy.; 808-637-4827; www.matsumotoshaveice.com)* near the town of Haleiwa for what's known as the best shave ice on the island.

The Matsumoto family has been serving up shave ice here (sometimes more than 1,000 a day) since 1951. Try the local favorite: shave ice, ice cream and red beans.

higher waves. Technically, this entire stretch of sand is Sunset Beach, but surfers divide it up according to surf break, with names like Gas Chambers, Back Doors, Off-The-Wall, Cloud Break, Pele's Followers, and the renowned Banzai Pipeline. Oh, and the sunsets here are awesome, too.

Waimea Bay – *South of Sunset Beach, on the north shore.* The beach at Waimea boasts the longest rideable surf break in the world. Spectators crowd the sands during the winter months when the surf is at its highest. Ironically, during the summer the water is generally calm and the beach is a fine swimming spot—but if the surf is up, be careful!

Makaha Beach Park – *South of Makua, on the west shore.* On the leeward side of the island, Makaha is a longtime favorite with island surfers, especially during the winter months when the winds kick up big waves.

Hawaii Tourism Authority/Kirk Lee Aeder

Waikiki Beach

Share the Waters★★

Follow a team of marine biologists to the untrammeled Leeward Coast. You'll board a catamaran and sail to where humpback whales breed and endangered spinner dolphins frolic. **Wild Side Specialty Tours** *(808-306-7273; www.sailhawaii.com)* takes small groups on its research trips to observe the entertaining humpbacks. You'll watch as the whales (as many as 6,000 migrate to Hawaiian waters) hurl out of the water and sing and chase each other as part of the mating ritual. Then don a pair of fins and a mask to swim alongside spinner dolphins—the most acrobatic of all dolphins—sea turtles, and schools of tropical fish. Along the way, you'll learn about sea creatures, habitat, and conservation.

Whale-watching season runs mid-December through April; snorkel trips are offered year-round. It's a 45-minute drive to the catamaran but they'll pick you up in Waikiki.

Take a Sunset Cruise★

There are few things more romantic than a sunset cruise along the Oahu coastline. You'll slip past world-famous Diamond Head *(see p112)* and along the sparkling Kohala Gold Coast, with the rolling Koolau mountains as a backdrop. Take your beloved out on the open deck, where you'll be caressed by balmy tropical winds and treated to a view of the postcard-pretty purple-and-pink-streaked sky. Watch the twinkling lights of Waikiki Beach and Honolulu dot the landscape, as the sun seems to head for the other side of the world.

Tea Traditions

Has all that Waikiki hustle and bustle got you frazzled? Here's a quick cure: participate in a tea ceremony at the **Urasenke Tea House** in Waikiki *(245 Saratoga Rd.; 808-923-3059)*. The soothing, centuries-old ceremony offers a peek into the Japanese "Way of Tea." The ceremony, including an informative video presentation, is held on Wed and Fri from 10am to noon. Everyone is welcome *($3 donation suggested)*.

FOR FUN

Luau, Anyone?

This outdoor feast—complete with a kalua pig roasted in an *imu* (underground oven)—may be the best way to hear traditional tunes and sample typical Island foods. Expect to be served poi (taro-root paste, offered fresh or fermented), *laulau* (steamed meat, fish and taro leaves wrapped in ti leaves), *lomi-lomi salmon* (salted salmon mixed with tomatoes and onions) and *haupia* (coconut pudding).

Contact the **Oahu Visitors Bureau** *(877-525-6248; www.visit-oahu.com)* for a list of companies offering cruises. Most feature dinner and entertainment, and cost from $50 to $60.

Waimea Valley★★

59-864 Kamehameha Hwy., Haleiwa. 808-638-7766. www.wai meavalley.net. Open year-round daily 9am–5pm. Closed Jan 1 & Dec 25 (park closes at 3pm on Thanksgiving Day & Dec 31). $10 adults, $5 children (ages 4–12).

Waimea Valley Botanical Gardens

This tranquil 1,875-acre oasis, nestled in the lush Waimea Valley on Oahu's north shore, offers a peaceful escape from the concrete jungle and never-ending action of Honolulu and Waikiki Beach. It's also a great place to learn about ancient Hawaiian culture and natural history; there's a spiderweb of nature trails to meander on your own, some leading to archeological sites.

Botanical Gardens – You could spend hours roaming the park's colorful gardens, including more than 5,000 species of plants spread across 36 themed areas and covering 150 acres. Pick up a map and pamphlet at the visitor center to help guide you through the gardens; plants from around the world, including native Hawaiian collections and rare species, are identified with small signs. Or sign up for one of the guided tours, including wildlife walks and native Hawaiian plant walks. There are arts and crafts demonstrations, too.

Waimea Falls – Be sure to save time for a walk to Waimea Falls, the spectacular centerpiece of the preserve. A 3.5-mile self-guided hike leads to the 40-foot-high falls. Stand back and take a good look: do you think the falls form the shape of a woman? Some locals think so and have thus nicknamed the waters "Wahine Falls" (*wahine* is the Hawaiian word for woman). Pack your bathing suit; swimming in the crystal-clear pools is allowed when the weather and winds cooperate (lifeguards are on duty).

MUST DO

OAHU

Snorkel at Hanauma Bay★★★

Off Hwy. 72, Hanauma Bay (10mi east of Wailkiki). 808-396-4229. www.honolulu.gov/parks/facility/hanaumabay/welcome.htm. Open Jun–Aug Wed–Mon 6am–7pm (second and fourth Sat until 10pm). Rest of the year Wed–Mon 6am–6pm. Closed Tue. $5 (free for children ages 12 and under).

©Philip Coblentz/Brand X Pictures

Crystal-clear, turquoise-blue Hanauma Bay is one of the best places in the islands for snorkeling. The underwater treasure, now a designated marine conservation district, teems with some 400,000 tropical fish (more than 150 species)

Touring Tip

Alas, Hanauma Bay is not an undiscovered gem. Located on the southeastern shore of Oahu, about a 30-minute drive from Honolulu, this place is hugely popular. The park now limits the number of people admitted each day; arrive early in the morning to snag a parking spot and admittance. Facilities at the beach park include restrooms, showers, concessions and equipment rentals.

Made in Hawaii

Visiting Oahu in late August? You're in luck. The annual three-day Made in Hawaii Festival showcases Hawaii-made items, created by more than 300 companies—all displayed under one roof at the Neal S. Blaisdell Center in Honolulu *(777 Ward Ave).* There are cooking demos and live music, too. *For more information, contact the Hawaii Food Industry Association at 808-533-1292 or www.madeinhawaiifestival.com.*

that swim around the impressive reef and coral formations. Don your masks and fins (rentals are available on-site) and swim with colorful parrotfish, tangs, Moorish idols, butterfly fish and more. A snowy white beach ringing the half-mile horseshoe-shape bay, and flanking volcanic cliffs are scenic bonuses.

Marine Education Center – When you need a break from snorkeling and swimming, check out the Marine Education Center at the park, featuring programs and exhibits on the history of the bay and conservation efforts.

Camping on Oahu

Oahu has several state and county park campgrounds that sure beat the price of an upscale hotel. State park campgrounds include the 5,228-acre **Malaekahana Beach** *(off Hwy. 83)* and the 110-acre **Kahana Valley** *(52-222 Hwy. 83, Kahana),* both with swimming, picnic areas and hiking trails. Near Honolulu, **Keaiwa Heiau State Recreation Area** *(end of Aiea Heights Dr., Aiea)* offers rustic camping, and **Sand Island State Recreation Area** *(end of Sand*

FOR FUN

Hawaii Tourism Authority/Sri Maiava Rusden

Island Access Rd., off Hwy. 92, Honolulu) offers 14 acres of camping along the coast.

Golf Oahu

Decisions, decisions. Oahu brims with top-notch golf courses, so where does a discerning duffer begin? You can't go wrong with these highly-rated links:

Makaha – *84-626 Makaha Valley Road, Waianae. 808-695-9544. www. makaharesort.net.* With stunning views of the Makaha Valley and towering, volcanic cliffs, this classic 7,077-yard course is one of the prettiest on Oahu.

Hawaii Kai – *8902 Kalanianaole Hwy., Honolulu. 808-395-2358. www. hawaiikaigolf.com.* You'll revel in splendid views of the Pacific Ocean and Makapuu Cliffs at this 6,614-yard, 18-hole championship course.
Koolau Golf Club – *45-550 Kionaole Rd., Kaneohe. 808-247-7088. www.koolaugolfclub.com.* Ready for a real challenge? The US Golf Association deems Koolau the toughest course in the country.
Koolina Golf Course – *92-1220 Aliinui Dr., Kapolei. 808-676-5300. www.koolinagolf.com.* This 6,867-yard Ted Robinson design is ranked among the top courses on the island.
Turtle Bay Resort – *57-091 Kamehameha Hwy., Kahuku. 808-293-8574. www.turtlebayresort.com.* Boasting 36 holes of championship golf, including an 18-hole course designed by Arnold Palmer and Ed Seay, Turtle Bay challenges all skill levels with five to six sets of tees on each hole.

Soar the skies

For an unbeatable birds-eye view, hop aboard a seaplane. Island Seaplane (*808-836-6273, www. islandseaplane.com*), the only seaplane service on the island, offers a sky-high tour from Hanauma Bay to the North Shore, with

Touring Tip

All Oahu state parks charge $5 per campsite per night. Camping is allowed Friday through Wednesday nights, except at Sand Island, where camping is permitted Friday through Monday only. Permits are required *(obtain permits from the Division of State Parks, 1151 Punchbowl St., Room 131, Honolulu; 808-587-0300 or 808-768-3440; www.hawaiistateparks.org).*

Camping is free at several county beach parks on Oahu. *For more information on parks and for a list of locations where you can pick up the required permits, contact the Department of Parks and Recreation: 650 South King St., Honolulu; 808-523-4525; www.co.honolulu.hi.us/parks.*

MUST DO   OAHU

How Did Surfing Begin?

Surfboarding, or wave riding, was an integral part of the ancient Hawaiian culture. By the time Captain Cook arrived on the islands in 1778, surf boarding was widespread, and an important aspect of sacred and religious ceremonies and practices. However, when the Europeans came to settle in the islands, Hawaiian culture, including surfing, began to die out. By the turn of the 20C, surfing had all but disappeared. It wasn't until Jack London visited Waikiki and wrote about the sport in 1907, and Alexander Hume Ford founded the Hawaiian Outrigger Canoe Club in 1908, that surfing began its modern-day resurgence.

A few years later, Duke Paoa Kahanamoku put the sport of surfing on the map for good. Duke was a famous Olympic gold-medal swimmer—and avid surfer. Known as "the fastest swimmer alive," Duke used his fame to introduce the world

to surfing. Today, he's known as "the father of surfing," and you'll find tributes to him throughout the islands, including the famous Duke statue on Waikiki Beach and the popular Duke's Canoe Club bar and restaurant at the Outrigger Waikiki Hotel in Honolulu *(2335 Kalakaua Ave.; see p186)* and on the island of Kauai *(on Kalapaki Beach, in front of the Kauai Marriott Resort; 808-246-9599; www.dukeskauai.com).*

plenty of colorful commentary and anecdotes along the way. The plane departs from the same water runways used by the PanAm clipper ships, and flies across the same path the Japanese used to bomb Pearl Harbor.

Listen to the Royal Hawaiian Band

If you happen to be king and like music, what do you do? You create a band, by royal decree. That's what King Kamehameha III did in 1836, and the band plays on. Today the Royal Hawaiian Band is an agency of the city and county of Honolulu and the only full-time municipal band in the US. For a delightful earful of traditional island music, check out the band's free concerts, held Fridays from noon to 1pm at the Coronation Pavilion at **Iolani Palace★★** *(S. King & Richard Sts.; see p124).* The band also plays several times a week at various loca-

tions throughout the city. *For more information and a schedule of appearances, call 808-922-5331 or check online at www. royalhawaiianband.com.*

Take a Hike

Get out of the bustling city and into the jungle! Oahu has an extensive system of hiking trails through tropical forests, and to waterfalls and mountain summits. **Popular hikes include** the Pu'u Ohia trail, an easy trek through tropical forest; Tantalus forest trails, leading to a 1,200-foot summit; the nine-mile Maunawili Trail; Diamond Head trail; the Aiea Loop with views into Halawa Valley; Manoa Falls through a bamboo rainforest to a 150-foot waterfall; and Maunawili Falls, a family-friendly, beginner's hike to a waterfall and swimming hole. Several tour operators offer guided hikes, a good way to learn more about the flora, fauna, and cultural history of the island. Try www.oahunaturetours.com.

FOR FUN

133

FOR KIDS

Aquariums, a hands-on kids' museum, a zoo, and an authentic working ranch! It's easy to keep *keiki* happy on Oahu.

Sea Life Park

Sea Life Park★★

41-202 Kalanianaole Hwy., Waimanalo. 866-365-7446. www.sealifeparkhawaii.com. Open year-round daily 10:30am–5pm. $29 adults, $19 children (ages 3–11).

Ever wonder what lurks beneath Hawaiian waters? Step into this popular attraction and you'll get a first-hand, close-up look. The oceanfront marine park sits on scenic Makapuu Point, 20 miles outside Honolulu on the windward coast. Just inside the gates, you'll see the impressive 300,000-gallon aquarium, home to more than 2,000 species of marine life. Watch as huge schools of neon-colored tropical fish, sea turtles, eels and sharks swim by in the 18-foot-high **Hawaiian Reef Tank**. Stop by the sea lion feeding pool and the sea turtle lagoon, then make your way to the stingray exhibit, where you can watch the slinky black creatures slide through the water—and touch them, if you wish.

Entertaining dolphin and sea lion shows are presented throughout the day, and the park offers a number of special tours.

Have you always wanted to train dolphins? Would you like to swim

Swim Little Turtles, Swim!

The sea turtle lagoon at the Sea Life Park on Oahu doubles as a breeding sanctuary for threatened Hawaiian green sea turtles. To date, 2,200 hatchlings have been produced in the park lagoon and released into the wild.

The cold-blooded reptile gets its name from the color of its body fat, which turns green from the algae it eats. Once plentiful on the islands and heavily hunted by natives, the Hawaiian green sea turtle is now protected by law. Over 90 percent of the nesting of these island reptiles now occurs inside the National Wildlife Refuge at French Frigate Shoals.

alongside a school of stingrays? Here's your chance; behind-the-scene programs are offered daily (for an extra fee).

Honolulu Zoo ★

In Kapiolani Park, 151 Kapahulu Ave. (between Diamond Head & Waikiki), Honolulu. 808-971-7171. www.honoluluzoo.org. Open year-round daily 9am–4:30pm. Closed Jan 1 & Dec 25. $8 adults, $4 youth (ages 13–17), $1 children (ages 6–12), free for under 5s.

Kids and animals—this is one combination where you can't go wrong! Make a beeline for the Diamond Head side of town to this small but sure-to-please zoo, home to more than 1,200 animals. The zoo stretches over 42 flat acres in Kapiolani Park; you can see the entire place in half a day—then, off to the beach! Kids and adults alike vote the **Kabuni Reserve** as their favorite area. This African Savannah habitat covers 12 acres, where you can walk along a path and peer at free-roaming zebra, rhinos, lions, hippos, giraffes, chimps and more. Don't miss the tropical forest, the Galapagos tortoises, and the reptile house. Chances are you haven't spotted Hawaii's state bird in the wild, but

Honolulu Zoo

you'll see them here; rare nene birds *(see p62)* waddle around the zoo, chirping happily.

Kualoa Ranch ★

49-560 Kamehameha Hwy., Kaaawa. 808-237-7321. www.kualoa.com. Open year-round daily 7:30am–5:30pm. Closed Jan 1 & Dec 25. Ranch and movie set tour, $19; other tours offered; prices vary, depending on activity.

Kualoa Ranch

The ropin', the ridin', the shootin'—yee haw! Play 'cowpoke' for a day at this authentic working ranch, sitting on 4,000 acres on Oahu's north shore, about an hour from Honolulu.

The property is stunning, encompassing three mountains and two valleys, spreading from steep mountain cliffs to the seashore. Of course, your kids won't care much about the views, but they will enjoy horseback riding (pony rides for ages 3–7), ATV trail rides, catamaran trips to ancient fish ponds, and ranch tours. If the scenery looks familiar, it's because Kualoa Ranch has been used as a backdrop for several movies, including *Jurassic Park*, *Mighty Joe*, *Pearl Harbor*, *Windtalkers*, and *Along Came Polly*.

Go Fly A Kite

Why not combine a day at the beach with some kite-flying? **Sandy Beach** on Oahu's east shore is considered the kite-flying capital of the islands. Look up and you'll see blue skies, wispy clouds, and a riot of colorful wings and tails. There's plenty of action in the water, here, too. The wild shore break and big swells make it a favorite among body boarders and surfers. Bring a picnic and enjoy the show!

Waikiki Aquarium★

In Queen Kapiolani Park, 2777 Kalakaua Ave., Honolulu. 808-923-9741. www.waquarium.org. Open year-round daily 9am–4:30pm. Closed Dec 25; limited hours Jan 1 & Thanksgiving Day. $9 adults, $4 youth (ages 13–17), $2 children (ages 5–12).

Dating back to 1904, the second-oldest public aquarium in the country showcases more than 2,500 underwater animals at its location on the Diamond Head end of Waikiki Beach. Here, you'll see slinky sea jellies, skinny moray eels, living corals, and giant, two-foot-long clams, the largest in the world.

Waikiki Aquarium

Waikiki Aquarium/University of Hawaii

Kids love the **Hunters on the Reef** exhibit, where they get a close look at hungry reef sharks circling the tank. The tide-pool area and the outdoor tank, home to a couple of endangered and oh-so-cute monk seals, are also popular.

Take in a show at the **Sea Visions Theater**, or sign up for day and night reef walks, behind-the-scenes programs, and diving and snorkeling trips.

🚸 Hawaii Children's Discovery Center

111 Ohe St., Honolulu. 808-524-5437. www.discovery centerhawaii.org. Open year-round Tue–Fri 9am–1pm, weekends 10am–3pm. Closed major holidays, and 2 wks. following Labor Day. $8 adults, $6.75 children (ages 1–17).

If you have little ones in tow and need to get out of the sun for a while, check out the Discovery Center. You'll find four galleries of please-touch exhibits where kids can pretend to be firefighters, bankers or mechanics, make rainbows, and learn about other cultures.

A Fishy Meal

Mealtime at the **Oceanarium Restaurant** at the Pacific Beach Hotel in Honolulu *(2490 Kalakaua Ave.; 808-921-6111; www.pacificbeachhotel.com)* is sure to entertain your little ones. The restaurant's centerpiece is a three-story, 280,000-gallon aquarium, showcasing more than 400 fish. Divers feed the fish during lunch and dinner hours for added excitement. Can anyone find the spotted eagle ray?

PERFORMING ARTS

The world-class city of Honolulu supports a thriving cultural and musical arts scene. Useful information can be found at www.hawaiistatetheatrecouncil.com.

Hawaii Opera Theater

Hawaii Opera Theater

Hawaii Opera Theater

987 Waimanu St., Honolulu. 800-836-7372. Box office: 808-596-7858. www.hawaiiopera.org. Season runs Jan–Mar. Ticket prices vary per performance.

Grand opera in the middle of the Pacific? You bet. The Hawaii Opera Theater, HOT for short, has never been hotter! Recent productions held at the 2,000-seat **Neil S. Blaisdell Concert Hall** have received international recognition.

Touring Tip
The best way to tap into local culture: time your visit to coincide with an "Only in Hawaii" event. Tops in this category include the annual Merrie Monarch Festival on the Big Island, the Ki Ho'alu Slack Key Guitar and Ukulele Concert series on Kauai, and the Friday concerts by the Royal Hawaiian Band on the grounds of Iolani Palace on Oahu. *See Calendar of Events (pp10–11) for other options.*

Hawaii Theater

1130 Bethel St., Honolulu. Box office: 808-528-0506. www.hawaiitheatre.com. One-hour guided tours of the performance hall are offered every Tuesday at 11am (subject to change). $5.

You'll find first-class music, theater, film and dance performances at Honolulu's historic Hawaii Theater. Built in 1922, the 1,400-seat hall, dubbed the "Pride of the Pacific," has been a landmark venue in downtown Honolulu for more than eight decades.

Honolulu Symphony Orchestra

777 Ward Ave., Honolulu. 808-524-0815. Box office: 808-792-2000. www.honolulusymphony.com. Season runs Sept–May. Ticket prices vary per performance.

Founded in 1900, this well-regarded group is the oldest American orchestra west of the Rockies. Lead conductor Andreas Delfs woos top international artists to the Neal S. Blaisdell Concert Hall, to perform classical works by Bernstein, Dvorak, Mozart, Gershwin and others. The symphony also pays tribute to the cultural roots of Hawaii, working the Chinese lute and Japanese taiko drums into the repertoire. The Grammy-nominated Honolulu Symphony Pops blends an exciting mix of classical and pop music.

SHOPPING

High-end fashion malls, designer boutiques, colorful open air vendors and giant flea markets will keep even serious shopaholics satiated.

Chinatown★★

West of Nuuanu Ave., between Ala Moana & Vineyard Blvds., Honolulu. 808-521-4934. www.chinatownhi.com. Outside vendors open year-round daily 8:30am–5pm.

This fascinating 15-block historic enclave—said to be the oldest Chinatown in the country—is a colorful, eclectic place to roam, shop and eat. The ethnic neighborhood, dating back more than 120 years, buzzes with energy and brims with local color and culture. Browse the sidewalk markets that overflow with exotic fruits, flowers (this is *the* place to buy a lei!) and foodstuffs.

When hunger strikes, stop at one of the more than 30 ethnic eateries, like **Legend Seafood**

Chinatown

Brigitta L. House/Michelin

Restaurant *(100 N. Beretania St.; 808-532-1868)* offering some of the best dim sum in the islands.

Celebrate Chinatown –
To really experience Chinatown, visit during one of the neighborhood's annual festivals. Here are a few to choose from:

- **Night in Chinatown** – Kick off the Chinese New Year at this annual street fair *(on Mauakea St., from Beretania St. to King St.)*, which features food, arts and crafts, music and dancing.

- **Narcissus Festival** – 808-533-31818 or www.ccchi.org/narcissus/index.html. Started in 1950 to showcase Chinese art and culture, the Narcissus Festival is the oldest ethnic festival in Hawaii. The celebration is held in conjunction with the Chinese lunar New Year.

- **Dragon Boat Festival** – 808-595-6417 or www.idealhawaii.com. Dragon boat races are the main reason to attend this traditional summertime event, held to drive off evil spirits. Crews in colorfully painted dragon-headed canoes challenge each other to the rhythm of beating drums.

Best Source for Aloha Wear

Established in 1963, **Hilo Hattie** *(808-535-6500; www.hilohattie.com)*, with stores scattered throughout the islands, remains one of the best places to buy Aloha wear and island-made fashions. For the widest selection and prices, visit the Nimitz Flagship Store and manufacturing facility in Honolulu *(700 N. Nimitz Highway; 808-535-6500; www.hilohattie.com)*. It's open daily from 8:30am to 6:30pm.

Take a Trolley

You want to shop, but the rest of your group wants to sunbathe. Go ahead, leave them the car and hop on one of the island's trolleys. The open-air trolleys travel from major hotels to the big malls in Honolulu and Waikiki, stopping at top attractions along the way. For schedules and routes, contact The Trolley Company *(808-593-2822; www.waikikitrolley.com)*. A one-day pass costs $27 and offers unlimited on-and-off boarding. You can pick up a **Waikiki Trolley Map Guide** at the Royal Hawaiian and Ala Moana malls, as well as at many hotels.

Ala Moana Shopping Center

Ala Moana Shopping Center★★

1450 Ala Moana Blvd., Waikiki. 808-973-9517. www.alamoana center.com. Open year-round Mon–Sat 9:30am–9pm, Sun 10am–7pm. Closed Dec 25.

Hawaii's largest open-air mall boasts more than 290 stores. Located in the heart of Waikiki, overlooking Ala Moana Beach Park, this shopping venue is always bustling. Serious shoppers will find retail biggies like Macy's and Neiman Marcus, as well as a collection of top-name designers—Escada, DKNY, Prada, Gucci, and Hermès. There are also several stores specializing in Hawaiian-made products and island wear. The outdoor space is opulently landscaped, and there are plenty of places to grab a bite to eat, from the food court to fine dining. The Ala Moana Shopping Shuttle runs from ten locations in Waikiki to the shopping center.

Aloha Stadium Swap Meet★★

Aloha Stadium, 99-500 Salt Lake Blvd., Honolulu. 808-486-6704. www.alohastadiumswapmeet.net. Open year-round Wed, Sat & Sun 6am–3pm. Closed Dec 25, and at 1pm on days when University of Hawaii football games are scheduled. $1 entry fee per buyer; under 11 free.

If you're looking for a bargain and consider haggling a sport, don't miss this popular outdoor flea market held outside the University of Hawaii's Aloha football stadium. It's one of the largest flea markets in the islands, with more than 700 vendors. Hordes of people gather around the stalls of vendors, bargaining for arts and crafts, souvenirs, housewares, ethnic food

Honolulu Fish Auction

Set your alarms and get up early to see the authentic, live Fish Auction, that's been held in Honolulu for more than half a century. The auctioneer walks down the rows of fish, while top chefs battle for the best prices. The lively auction is held Mon–Sat, from 5:30am, and lasts until all the fish are sold.

Sweet Souvenirs

If you're craving those chocolate-covered macadamia nuts, visit the **Menehune Mac Factory Gift Center** *(707-A Waiakamilo Rd.; 808-841-3344; www.menehune mac.com)*. Buy some for munching immediately (who can resist?), then stock up on handmade chocolates, kaiulani spices, Hawaiian pasta and island-made jams and jellies to take home.

Aloha Tower

© Aloha Tower Marketplace

souvenirs, housewares, ethnic food items, fine art, and knick-knacks. It's a fun atmosphere and a great place to rub elbows with the locals.

Aloha Tower Marketplace★

Pier 9, downtown Honolulu. 808-528-5700. www.alohatower.com. Shops open Mon–Sat 9am–9pm, Sun 9am–6pm. Special holiday hours apply Thanksgiving Day & Dec 25.

You can't miss this entertainment, dining and shopping complex, wrapped around the imposing **Aloha Tower★★** *(see p105)*. And you can't beat the location, sitting on downtown Honolulu's pretty oceanfront harbor.

This is a popular place to hang out, pick up souvenirs and sundries, and grab a bite to eat. Stores run the gamut from gift, apparel, home furnishings and jewelry shops. With its array of casual restaurants and bars, the marketplace is a lively place both day and night.

Royal Hawaiian Shopping Center

2201 Kalakaua Ave., Waikiki. 808-922-2299. www.royalhawaiian center.com. Open year-round daily 10am–10pm. www.shopwaikiki. com. Special holiday hours apply Thanksgiving Day & Dec 25.

Located in the heart of Waikiki, this mall recently received a much-needed multi-million dollar renovation. Within walking distance of most major hotels, this is now one of Hawaii's largest malls, stretching over two blocks with more than 110 shops and restaurants. Whatever you want, you'll find it here, from tacky to tony. Upscale designer boutiques are scattered among souvenir shops, arts and crafts, sundries and convenience stores. Check out the free Hawaiian cultural and arts programs, including demonstrations and lessons on hula, ukulele, lei-making, Hawaiian quilting, and lomilomi massage techniques. Torch-lighting ceremonies and free concerts are also held.

OAHU

MUST DO

NIGHTLIFE

Oahu heats up when the sun goes down, with the hottest nightlife of all the islands: Music, entertainment, dancing, eating—you name it!

 Barefoot Bar at Duke's Waikiki

2335 Kalakauna Ave., Waikiki Beach. 808-922-2268. www.dukeswaikiki.com.

This classic beach-boy bar, named in honor of surfing legend Duke Kahanamoku, is a longtime favorite with visitors and locals alike. It helps that the rollicking, open-air bar overlooks busy Waikiki Beach. The koa-wood-paneled room is chock-full of surfing memorabilia, including an outrigger canoe, antique surfboards and posters. It's a fun, casual vibe, with live Hawaiian entertainment nightly. For late-night noshing, there's a bar menu available until midnight with pizza, sandwiches, salads and burgers.

Chai's Island Bistro

Aloha Tower Marketplace, Pier 9, downtown Honolulu. 808-585-0011. www.chaisisland bistro.com.

Combine fabulous Hawaiian regional and Pacific Rim food with live, local entertainment and you have the winning combination of this upscale night spot on Waikiki Beach. Crowds flock to Chai's nightly to hear the hottest new musicians in Hawaii. Come later on Saturday night *(10pm–2am)* for DJ tunes, dancing on the outdoor patio and indoor dance floor, and free pupu (Hawaiian for "appetizers").

Light up the Night

Begin your evening by watching the traditional torch-lighting ceremony at Kuhio Beach Park in Waikiki. The nightly event begins with the blowing of a conch shell, as the first torches are lit. A hula dancing performance follows. Torch-lighting ceremonies are also held throughout Waikiki, at most of the major hotels and the Royal Hawaiian Shopping Center. Ceremonies usually begin around 6pm.

House Without a Key

2199 Kalia Rd., Halekulani Hotel, Honolulu. 808-923-2311. www.halekulani.com/dining/ house_without_a_key.

Even the most jaded local has to admit that this longtime indoor-outdoor venue is magical at sunset. Views of Diamond Head

Hawaii Tourism Japan

Blue Hawaii

Fabulous Freebies: free-for-all happenings in Honolulu

- The Royal Hawaiian Band plays at Iolani Palace, Fri noon–1pm and at Kapiolani Park, Sun 2pm–3pm
- Fireworks are held Fri night on the beach in front of the Hilton Hawaiian Village Resort
- On the first Fri, second Sat and third Thu of each month, Chinatown's art galleries extend their hours into the night and offer live music and drink specials

and the sherbet-colored dusk-lit skies are stunning. Add Hawaiian music and the hula, performed by talented locals, and you've got the perfect place to begin the evening. The sunset entertainment is held nightly from 5:30pm–8:30pm.

The Big Shows

Oahu certainly has its fair share of extravaganzas!

For a Waikiki beachfront luau, held at the **Royal Hawaiian** resort (see p185). 808-931-8383; www.royal-hawaiian.com.

Other luaus include local favorite **Germaine's Luau** (808-949-6626; www.germainesluau.com), the **Paradise Cove Luau** (808-842-5911; www.paradisecove hawaii.com) held on a beach on the west of the island, and the very authentic **Alii Luau** held at the Polynesian Cultural Center (800-367-7060; www.polynesia.com).

The exotic, multi-media **Creations-Polynesian Journey** show, held at the Sheraton Princess Kaiulani Hotel (808-922-5811; www.princess-kaiulani.com/de_creation.htm) features the dance and music of South Pacific islands, and includes an impressive Samoan fire knife dance.

The long-running and high-energy **Society of Seven LV** show, held at the Outrigger Waikiki on the Beach hotel (800-404-3391 or 808-926-3391; www.outriggeractivities.com; see p186), combines comedy, dance, and music.

Mai Tai Bar

1450 Ala Moana Blvd., in the Ala Moana Shopping Center, Honolulu. 808-947-2900. www.maitaibar.com.

You'll find plenty of action at this popular bar, perched over the Ala Moana Shopping Center. Voted best Happy Hour Bar, best Outdoor Bar, best Singles Bar, and best Place to listen to Live Music in Hawaii for the last two years running, it's a really great place to hear live music, and locals cram the airy, tropical bar during late afternoon Happy Hour—one of the best deals on the island. There's no excuse not to come here, sink into a comfy couch and sip one of their signature *mai tais*—made with three types of rum and fresh-squeezed fruit juices—as you listen to island rhythms.

Ocean Club

500 Ala Moana Blvd., Honolulu. 808-531-8444. Minimum entrance age 23.

Dress to the nines to visit this ultra-sleek restaurant-club open until 4am. The downtown venue sports rich mahogany woods, tile floors, and steel accents and is a hot spot for late night dancing to DJ-spun hip-hop and top 40s. The bar draws a hip, under-30 crowd.

MUST DO   OAHU

SPAS

You'll find some of the most lavish spas in the country, with lush, tropical gardens, waterfalls, and the Pacific Ocean as their backdrops.

Spa Suites

Kahala Resort, 5000 Kahala Ave., Honolulu. 808-739-8938. www.kahalaresort.com/spa.

You can't beat the soothing, private ambience at this unique spa at the Kahala Hotel & Resort, ten minutes from bustling Waikiki. Former hotel guest suites have been carefully converted into spacious treatment rooms. You'll be escorted through gardens to your private room, with changing area, infinity-edged bath, shower, and a small, private garden terrace (to relax in before and after your treatments). Most services begin with a traditional foot ritual, including a soak, sea salt exfoliation and mosturizer. Then, indulge in one of their luxe treatments, like the Kua Lani back, face and scalp massage, a detoxifying body wrap with warmed Hawaiian algae, or the volcanic mud envelopment.

Spa Suites, Kahala Resort

Kahala Resort

Ihilani Spa

JW Marriott Ihilani Resort at Ko Olina, 92-1001 Olani St., Kapolei. 808-679-3321 or 808-679-0079. www.ihilani.com.

Ihilani means "heavenly splendor," an apt name for this 35,000-square-foot sanctuary on Oahu's sunny western shore. Spend a few hours here (go ahead, make it a day!), getting a Maui ginger sugar body scrub, a green-tea detoxifying wrap or a seaweed mask, followed by a four-handed lomilomi massage. The spa is known for its authentic thalassotherapy, a seawater-jet massage, coupled with pure colored light and essential oils, designed to de-stress body and mind. In between treatments, you can relax in steam rooms and saunas, take a lap in the pool, or a plunge into one of the Roman baths (bathing suits optional).

SpaHalekulani

Halekulani Hotel, 2199 Kalia Rd., Honolulu. 800-367-2343. www.halekulani.com.

This small but tranquil spa, located at the plush Halekulani Hotel, combines treatments from a variety of South Pacific islands. Each room features a private terrace, fronting a swath of ocean and sandy beach. You'll begin with the pre-treatment foot pounding. Next choose from a menu of exotic treatments, like the Polynesian Nonu massage (using warm stones and medium pressure), the Thai yoga massage,

Na Hoola Spa

the cleansing Hibiscus body wrap, or the Tahitian coconut hair and scalp massage.

Na Hoola Spa

Hyatt Regency Waikiki, 2424 Kalakaua Ave., Honolulu. 808-923-1234. www.waikiki-hyatt.com.

This two-story, 10,000-square-foot spa, the largest on Waikiki, offers a peaceful oasis from the bustling beach scene below. You'll find 19 treatment rooms as well as a sauna, steam showers, and a couple's massage room—everything you need to ease your tired bones. Feeling a bit jet-lagged? Take a signature Hawaiian sea-salt jet bath. If your skin's feeling parched from the tropical sun, consider the spa's Polynesian body scrub, done with Hawaiian sea salt and kukui-nut oil.

Plantation Spa

Waikiki Outrigger on the Beach Hotel, 2335 Kalakaua Ave., Honolulu. 866-926-2880. www.waikikiplantationspa.com.

Take your time and savor the views from this lofty spa, occupying the penthouse level of the Waikiki Outrigger on the Beach.

The rooftop terrace, in a simple Zen-garden setting, offers bird's eye views of the Honolulu skyline and Pacific Ocean. For a parched, sun-dried body, try the Papaala polish, after a lavender spritz, you'll be drenched with cooling aloe vera and cucumber gels. The aromatherapy facials include a lava stone massage and volcanic mud mask.

Spa Luana

Turtle Bay Resort, 57-091 Kamehameha Hwy., Kahuku. 808-447-6868. www.turtlebay resort.com.

Hawaiians have long believed in the healing powers of sea water. This spa will make a believer out of you, too. The watery wildernesss setting, including outdoor treatment rooms overlooking the wild, rocky North Shore coastline, makes this a worthy destination.

Book a makai massage and have the therapist throw open the cabana's oceanfront flap.

LANAI ★

Billing itself as the "most enticing" island, tiny Lanai is central in the chain, with Molokai and Maui to the north and Kahoolawe to the east. Visitor information: 800-947-4774 or www.visitlanai.net. A ferry service to Lanai is available from Lahaina on Maui's west coast.

Formed by a single volcano, Lanai boasts stretches of white sandy beaches, pristine bays, and cool, pine-shrouded mountaintops. A series of gulches snakes down the island's east side. To the west, you'll see towering sea cliffs—some 1,000-feet tall—rising from remote Kaumalapau Harbor. If you're adventurous, a four-wheel-drive vehicle will take you across some of the island's undeveloped 80,000 acres of countryside and through tropical jungles. Scuba divers come to explore the legendary **Cathedral Ledges★** *(see p153)*, while adventurers head up the **Munro Trail★★** *(see p150)* to 3,370-foot Lanaihale, the island's highest peak. In truth, though, most people come here to be pampered at the island's two luxury resorts, the **Lodge at Koele** and the Four Seasons at **Manele Bay** *(see p186)*. After Boston businessman James Dole purchased

Fast Facts

- Measuring 18 miles long and 13 miles wide, Lanai is Hawaii's sixth-largest island.
- Only 5,000 people live on Lanai.
- Pineapple king James Dole purchased Lanai in 1922 for $1.1 million.
- Today about 96% of the island of Lanai is privately owned and developed as an upscale resort.
- You won't find a single traffic light on the island of Lanai.

the island in 1922, Lanai became home to the world's largest pineapple plantation. **Lanai City** was built in 1924 by the Hawaiian Pineapple Company, later known as Dole Food Company. Nestled on the top of a 1,620-foot mountain plateau, Lanai City now contains the majority of the island's 5,000 residents. Yet it remains, like the rest of the island, small, quaint and very laid-back. The Hawaiian corporation of Castle

Castle and Cooke Resorts

Manele Bay

Demons, Demons Everywhere

Legend has it that Lanai was once an evil place, overrun by demons. It was not until the demons were driven out by Kaululaau, the exiled son of a West Maui king, that people finally came to live on Lanai.

& Cooke later bought the pineapple plantation, retaining Dole's name. When market demand for Lanai pineapples plummeted in the 1990s, the company turned to high-end tourism, plowing under thousands of acres of the former pineapple plantation and developing the land with two posh hotels

and two golf courses.

Lanai lures two types of travelers: Adventure-seekers love the prime snorkeling and diving; the shallow waters and offshore reefs offer some of the best snorkeling and diving in Hawaii. And, with only 33 paved roads, there are many rugged and remote sites to visit, many accessible only by four-wheel drive vehicles. Off-road driving enthusiasts will love it here! Luxury lovers love Lanai for its two upscale resorts. Of course, you can play hard all day and luxuriate at night. Those in search of adventure, seclusion and upscale sybaritic pleasures will find it all on Lanai.

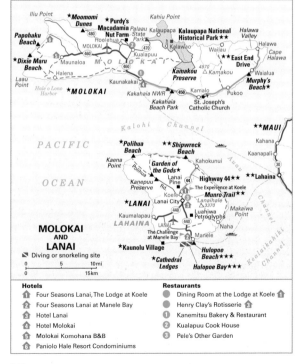

MOLOKAI AND LANAI

Diving or snorkeling site

0 — 5 — 10mi
0 — 15km

Hotels
1. Four Seasons Lanai, The Lodge at Koele
2. Four Seasons Lanai at Manele Bay
3. Hotel Lanai
4. Hotel Molokai
5. Molokai Komohana B&B
6. Paniolo Hale Resort Condominiums

Restaurants
- Dining Room at the Lodge at Koele
- Henry Clay's Rotisserie
1. Kanemitsu Bakery & Restaurant
2. Kualapuu Cook House
3. Pele's Other Garden

BEACHES

Many off Lanai's prettiest beaches are secluded, rugged, and treacherous. Hulopoe and Puu Pehe are the best for swimming.

Hulopoe Beach★★★

Hulopoe Beach is located next to the Manele Bay Hotel off Manele Rd./Hwy. 440 on the south end of the island.

Castle and Cooke Resorts
Hulopoe Beach

Considered one of the top beaches in the US, this popular stretch of white sand on Lanai's south shore draws crowds of swimmers, sunbathers and snorkelers. (Daily excursion boats from Maui land here.) The crystal-clear waters and shallow offshore reefs make it one of the best places in the islands to snorkel *(see p151)*. To the left of the beach is **Puu Pehe Rock**, also known as Sweetheart Rock. (Ask a local to tell you the Sweetheart Rock story; *see box, left*). Facilities include restrooms, showers and a picnic area with grills.

Sweetheart Rock

The legend goes that this rock takes its name from a tragic incident. Long ago, a Lanai warrior kidnapped a young, beautiful Maui girl and hid her on this rock. While the warrior was away, a storm blew in and washed the girl into the roiling surf, where she drowned. Heartbroken, the warrior flung himself from the cliff into his own watery grave.

Shipwreck Beach★★

At the end of Keomuku Rd. (Rte. 44), 8mi northeast of Lanai City.

This is a great place to walk, search for shells and driftwood, take in the salt air, and listen to the rhyth-

Castle and Cooke Resorts
Shipwreck Beach

BEACHES

147

Rock Art

While you're in the area of Shipwreck Beach, be sure to go see the petroglyphs, or rock carvings, at the end of Highway 44 *(when the paved road ends, take the north branch sand road all the way to the way to the end)*. Follow the trail, marked with white paint on the rocks, to a cluster of stones—many of which are etched with ancient drawings. You'll see lots of primitive images of men, women and children engaged in a variety of activities, such as surfing, fishing and hunting. Dogs, brought to the islands by the first Polynesians, and deer, brought from India in the mid-1800s, are also depicted.

mic hiss of the surf. The beach lines the island's northeast shore, stretching from Kahokunui at the end of Highway 44 to Polihua Beach to the northwest. Ancient Hawaiians called this eight-mile span of beach Kaiolohia, or "choppy seas."

Today it's the site of a number of shipwrecks, beginning with American and British ships in the early 19C. You'll still see remnants of ship hulls and other debris here; one of the most prominent is the rusting hulk of a World War II vessel, forever grounded on the reef offshore. The water isn't great for swimming—it's too muddy and rough—but nature-lovers will enjoy the wild, pristine surroundings.

Polihua Beach★

On the north coast, at the end of dirt Polihua Rd., beyond the Garden of the Gods (for directions and touring tip, see p151).

Polihua, meaning "eggs nest" or "bay of eggs," was named for the large numbers of sea turtles that once nested on this beach. After nearly becoming extinct, the sea turtles are starting to return to Polihua to nest—if you do see them, please remember to keep your distance. Forget about swimming here—the waters are too dangerous—but the wild, rugged character of the beach, with its crashing surf and solitude, is worth the drive to Lanai's north coast.

Polihua Beach

MUST SEE LANAI

NATURAL SITES

With only one town, and just 33 miles of paved roads, much of Lanai's stunning landscape remains pristine.

Petroglyph Sites

Without a written language, ancient Hawaiians used rock carvings—known as **petroglyphs**—to record their experiences. Tiny Lanai is home to three ancient petroglyph sites. *For driving directions to these sites, contact* **Destination Lanai** *(800-947-4774 or www.visitlanai.net).*

- At the end of a dirt road on the northwestern tip of the island, you'll find **Kaena Point**, Lanai's largest *heiau* (ancient place of worship).
- On the island's south shore, west of **Hulopoe Beach★★★**

(see p147), are the ruins of **Kaunolu Village★**, an ancient Hawaiian fishing village abandoned in the mid-19C. Here you can see the remains of Halulu Heiau, and a variety of petroglyphs on the surrounding boulders and rock walls.

- On a hillside overlooking the Palawai Basin are the **Luahiwa petroglyphs**, Lanai's largest concentration of ancient rock drawings, or kaha kii, carved in a number of large boulders scattered in the field *(off Hwy. 440, south of Lanai City).*

SCENIC DRIVES

See map p 146.

Highway 44★★

Begin in Lanai City, and take Hwy. 44 north.

This eight-mile drive, along Lanai's northeast coast, packs a lot of splendid scenery into its short distance. Also called Keomuku Road, the paved, two-lane byway, one of only two paved highways on Lanai, heads north out of Lanai City, past the Lodge at Keole. You'll enter a neon-green rain forest, backed by misty mountains. Along the way, there are turn-offs for the **Munro Trail★★** and the **Garden of the Gods** *(see p151).*

The road makes a final descent toward scenic **Shipwreck Beach★★** *(see p147).* This is a great spot to

Rent a Jeep

You'll need to rent a hefty, four-wheel-drive vehicle at the airport to explore the back (and muddy!) roads of Lanai, and the off-road/backroad scenery is worth the extra cost of a jeep. Try **Dollar Rent-A-Car**. *1036 Lanai Ave. 808-565-7227 or 800-800-3665. www.dollar.com.*

Castle and Cooke Resorts

When in Hawaii…

…Do as the Hawaiians do. Ancient Hawaiians revered nature, and respect for the land still holds a strong place in the lives of the Islanders. Treat all property with respect while visiting, especially sacred sites and natural areas. Don't touch anything, or leave litter behind. Other local customs include removing shoes before entering a private home, and obeying the speed limit (this is an easy-going place!). Don't pat children on the head, as the head is considered to be a sacred part of the body. Is it okay to say "aloha" if you're not Hawaiian? Sure, everybody does (aloha works for both "hello" and "goodbye"). Mahalo ("thank you") is handy, too.

get out and explore; you'll find remnants of old shipwrecks and fabulous coastal scenery here.

Munro Trail★★

Off Hwy. 44, near the Lodge at Koele.

If you've rented a four-wheel-drive vehicle (and you should), don't miss driving this bumpy dirt road to Lanai's highest point. The Munro Trail, located off Highway 44, is one of Lanai's most popular driving excursions, with exceptional views from its 3,370-foot summit. The trail is named after George Munro, who planted the tall Cook Pines in the early 1900s along the ridge of the mountains. The trees were planted to draw water from the clouds,

releasing it into the underground aqueducts, thus providing fresh water for the island.

The seven-mile trail zigzags up Lanaihale Mountain, then back down to the Palawai Basin, with lots of lookouts along the way. Chances are, it will be drizzling in the cloud-shrouded mountains, which only adds to the ambience.

Touring Tip

Be sure to check on the condition of the unpaved roads of Munro Trail and to the Garden of the Gods *(see p151)* before driving on them. When you're driving on Munro Trail, stay on the main road; it's easy to get lost on the spider web of trails and dirt roads leading off the beaten path.

Munro Trail

Castle and Cooke Resorts

GARDENS

Undeveloped Lanai has no formal public gardens but an extraordinary natural landscape to explore.

Keahiakawelo

Keahiakawelo

Hawaii Tourism Japan

225 B3 Polihua Rd., 6mi northwest of Lanai City. (Polihua Rd. starts just beyond the Lodge at Koele.) 866-268-7459. www.hawaiiweb. com/lanai. Open year-round daily 24 hours.

Dubbed the **Garden of the Gods**, this rugged, lunar-like landscape of randomly scattered volcanic boulders is indeed eerily stunning. Visit at sunrise or sunset, when the gold-tinged sky seems to illuminate the rocks from within. Seems like the perfect place for a UFO landing...

Touring Tip

The road to reach Keahiakawelo, Polihua Road, is a rutted dirt trail; you'll need a four-wheel-drive vehicle to navigate it. Call before you go; if there's been a recent rain, the road may be closed. Allow about an hour for your visit, and make sure you have plenty of gas before setting out—there are no facilities along this route.

HISTORIC SITES

Petroglyphs, ancient villages, former temples, shipwrecks and sacred sites dot the landscape, many in remote, rugged areas.

Kaunolu Village★

On the southwest coast. From Lanai City, take Hwy. 440 toward Kaumalapau; turn left onto Kaupili Rd. and go south to Kaunolu Trail.

Ready for an adventure? Put on your walking shoes and rent a hefty four-wheel-drive vehicle for this trek to an old fishing village on Lanai's southwest coast. The area is said to contain one of the best collections of ancient Hawaiian ruins in the islands, and if you look hard enough, you'll find crumbled house foundations and parts of buildings, as well as ruins of the Halulu Heiau temple. You won't have any problem spotting the impressive 1,000-foot-high sea cliffs. Look for Kahekili's Jump at the top of the stone wall, where early Hawaiian warriors would amuse the chief by jumping off the 90-foot-high ledge. Today it's the site of cliff-diving competitions. **Note:** Kaunolu Village is registered as a National Historical Landmark and visitors should not touch the excavated finds.

FOR FUN

Venture away from the resorts to see the best of Lanai, from its remote backroads scenery, underwater caves and ledges, and crystal clear bays.

Drive the Backroads★★

If you really want to see the best of Lanai's scenery, you'll have to brave its bumpy backroads. Stay on the road more traveled and you'll miss the heart of this tiny island. In fact, only 30 miles of Lanai's 141 square miles are paved; the rest are open for the adventurous to explore. Lanai offers more than 100 miles of unpaved, rough roads to travel, with spectacular views and remote vistas. Four-wheel-drive rental vehicles and road maps are available at the airport.

Don't miss a trip through the **Kanepuu Preserve**, about five miles northwest of Lanai City *(Polihua Rd, the dirt route leading to the preserve, is just beyond the Lodge at Koele)*. The 590-acre preserve boasts a large collection of native Hawaiian plants.

Continue about a mile on the Polihua Road to the **Garden of the**

Brigitta L.House/Michelin

Gods *(see p151)*, a bizarre stand of nature-sculpted rock formations. From here, strap on those seat belts and follow the dusty, dirty, rock-strewn road across the island to windswept **Polihua Beach★** *(see p148)*, a favorite sea turtle nesting ground on the north shore. You won't be disappointed: the beach here is wild, rugged and hauntingly beautiful.

Pull! Aim! Fire!

If you're looking for a unique experience (or just want to practice your rifle shooting), check out the **Lanai Pine Sporting Clays** *(Hwy. 44, North Central Lanai, just past mile marker 1; 808-559-4600; www.claytargetsonline.com/club. php/450)*.

Located on the picturesque plains of Mahana, on the north side of the island, this 14-station clay-shooting course welcomes both first-timers and experienced shooters. If you've never tried clay shooting, this is the place. Beginners can sign up for a 45-minute introductory lesson.

Castle and Cooke Resorts

MUST DO

LANAI

OUTDOOR FUN

Adventurous travelers love Lanai for its top-notch snorkeling, diving, and remote and rugged four-wheel driving.

Snorkeling at Hulopoe Bay★★★

Hulopoe Bay is located next to the Manele Bay Hotel off Manele Rd./Hwy. 440 (7mi south of Lanai City). The adjacent beach park has restrooms and showers.

Ultra-clear waters and abundant (and friendly!) fish make Hulopoe Bay on Lanai's south shore one of the best snorkeling spots in the islands. The protected marine conservation area features a shallow reef just offshore and lots of large tide pools, creating some great marine animal-watching opportunities.

Castle and Cooke Resorts

Head to the rocky sides of the beach for the best snorkeling; here, you'll find plenty of neon-colored coral and reef fish. If you arrive at Hulopoe early in the morning, you may see spinner dolphins frolicking offshore.

Scuba Diving at Cathedral Ledges★

Off the western edge of Holupoe Bay, next to the Manele Bay Hotel off Hwy. 440 (7mi south of Lanai City).

Green sea turtles, white-tipped reef sharks, spinner dolphins, octopi, eagle rays, hundreds of rare tropical fish, and more; the waters surrounding Lanai swim with marine life, a natural aquarium that draws scuba divers from around the country. Divers flock here to explore underwater ledges, arches, caves and lava tubes, home to thousands of neon-colored fish, sea creatures and reef corals. A popular place to dive is the **Cathedrals**, a large underwater amphitheater resting 60 feet

Cliff Diving

Legend has it that Kahekili, chief of Lanai during the 18C, challenged his followers by leaping 90 feet off the sacred cliffs at Kaunolu into the waters of the Pacific Ocean. For decades, **lele kawa** (cliff diving) was an honored Hawaiian tradition, a way for ancient island warriors to prove their courage and loyalty, and to honor the gods. Today, Lanai, considered the birthplace of cliff diving, is a favorite locale for the **Red Bull World Cliff-Diving Championship Tour**, where the best cliff divers compete for the international title on Kaunolu Point on the island's south shore.

OUTDOOR FUN

Day Trips to Lanai

Trilogy (888-225-6284; www.sailtrilogy.com), based on Maui, offers several popular day trips to Lanai. The sunrise and sunset sails include snorkeling at Hulopoe Bay Marine Sanctuary and an historical tour of the island led by a local guide. Tours depart from Lahaina Harbor on the west coast of Maui.

below the water's surface, just outside the western edge of Holupoe Bay. Light shines through the openings of this massive lava formation, creating the effect of a cathedral. Bright colors streak the lava walls and eels hide in the crevices.

Golf Lanai

Lanai's two resort courses, The Experience at Koele and The Challenge at Manele Bay, have both received oodles of accolades and are consistently ranked as two of the top resort courses in the country, if not the world.

The Challenge at Manele Bay – *Four Seasons Resort Lanai at Manele Bay, 7mi south of Lanai City on Manele Rd./Hwy. 440. 808-565-2222. www.fourseasons.com/manelebay/golf.html.* Take the Challenge at this Jack Nicklaus-designed course, across gorges and ravines with

sweeping ocean vistas from every hole. The rugged 7,039-yard, Par 72 course rolls over ancient lava fields, with jaw-dropping coastline views. Three holes perch on the cliffs of Hulopoe Bay, using the Pacific Ocean as a water hazard!

The Experience at Koele – *Four Seasons Resort Lanai The Lodge at Koele, .5mi north of Lanai City on Hwy. 430. 808-565-4653. www.fourseasons.com/koele/golf.html.* Greg Norman and renowned golf course architect, Ted Robinson, laid out this 163-acre course, which meanders through a highland landscape of woodsy ravines, and large stands of koa, ecalyptus and distinctive Cook pines. There are views of Maui and Molokai from the 2,000-foot plateau, seven lakes, and cascading streams and waterfalls, with mountain and ocean views, to boot.

The Challenge at Manele Bay

FOR KIDS

Forget formal museums, amusement parks, and entertainment centers; outdoor recreation reigns in Lanai's giant natural playground.

Outdoor Adventures

Lanai's 140 square miles of sandy shoreline, secluded bays, green valleys, lofty plateaus and dense forests make for some great recreation—perfect for outdoor enthusiasts and adventurous families. You'll definitely want to get out and play!

Riding in Lanai

Castle and Cooke Resorts

- **Take a hike** through the forest and valleys of the island's pretty uplands. Parents will appreciate the lofty scenery of the sheer valley walls and the open vistas, with the islands of Maui and Molokai on the horizon, while kids will enjoy running along the trail, through the leafy, enchanted forest. A guided 5-mile tour is offered at the **Lodge at Koele** *(.5mi north of Lanai City on Hwy. 430; see p188).* Private hikes are also available.

- Sign up for a **guided horseback ride** through the countryside. Equestrians young and old will enjoy this excursion; even the little tykes can hop in the saddle for a gentle ride around the corral. *Call the stables at the Lodge at Koele for more information and reservations: 808-565-4000.*

Adventure Lanai EcoCenter

Door-to-door pickup. 808-565-7373; www.adventurelanai.com.

The owners and outfitters at this company love showing off their favorite island and introducing you to some wild adventure. They offer guided 4x4 treks, kayaking and snorkeling adventures, surfing lessons, and more. The 4-hour kayak eco excursion includes instruction, equipment, and a paddle to a favorite snorkeling spot to view sea turtles, dolphins, whales, and more.

Morning surfing safari – Ready to ride the waves? This 4-hour morning surfing safari takes beginners of all ages to a secluded beach to learn how to surf. Or, you can try your hand at kayak surfing.

Prefer 4x4? – Private 4x4 adventure tours of the island—perfect for families—include Cook Island along the Munro Trail, Garden of the Gods, and Shipwreck Beach.

Outdoor Kids'-only Programs – The EcoCenter offers snorkeling, swimming, kayaking, body boarding, and surfing for kids only.

Rental – If your family would rather go it alone, the EcoCenter provides a plethora of rental sports equipment and 4x4 vehicles. The company will transport you to and from all activities and deliver equipment to your door.

155

SPAS

Bad news: there's not a lot to choose from on Lanai.
Good news: what is here is great!

The Spa at Manele Bay

At the Four Season Lanai at Manele Bay (7mi south of Lanai City on Manele Rd./Hwy. 440). 808-565-2000. www.fourseasons.com/manelebay.

Now this is the life! Reserve the open-air cabana at the ultra-luxe spa at Four Seasons Lanai at Manele Bay for your personal massage.

The private outdoor room is tucked in a corner between the resort's too-blue pool and the open seas, where you can listen to the sound of the surf while the therapist kneads your tired muscles (no piped-in nature CDs needed, here!). If you prefer, there's also the Garden Hale outdoor room, set amidst lush greenery, exotic flowers and cascading waterfalls. For

The Spa at Manele Bay

© Four Seasons

the ultimate experience, the spa will reopen its doors after closing hours for your private use.

From Poi to Pineapple: Eating Hawaiian-style

Talk about a melting pot! It seems as if many Hawaiian food treats incorporate a dollop of several cultures and a dash of island ingredients. One example: Spam musubi, which consists of sticky rice topped by Spam and wrapped in dried seaweed. Introduced to Hawaii by the military during World War II, good old Spam (spiced ham in a can) remains a favorite here. Hawaiians eat more of the stuff than anyone else in the world! The ubiquitous plate lunch, a local favorite at roadside stands, consists of white rice, pasta salad, and an entrée—perhaps Chinese-style chicken in soy sauce, Japanese teriyaki, curry stew, fried fish, or even an American hamburger.

Poi is uniquely Hawaiian. Made out of pounded taro root, this purplish, pasty stuff is said to have special healing properties. If you're not tempted by poi, you may well want to sample **shave ice**, an old-fashioned treat from the days when islanders would shave ice into powder and flavor it with fruit juice. (Remember, it's shave ice, not shaved ice!)

Hawaii Toourism Japan

MOLOKAI ★

Untouristy. Relaxed. Authentically Hawaiian. These are the words that Molokai residents use when describing their island. "My dad used to bring us to Molokai from Oahu to teach us how to drive, because there are no traffic lights!" one woman told us. That's Molokai!
Visitor information: 808-553-5221 or www.molokai-hawaii.com.

This 38-mile-long island was once the province of *kahuna* (priests) whose religious practices included human sacrifice. The island was considered sacred then. Now a grove of kukui trees (which are sacred themselves) marks the burial site of Lani Kauli, one of the most powerful kahunas. Molokai was also the home of Father Damien, the Belgian Roman Catholic priest who devoted his life to caring for the victims of Hansen's Disease (aka leprosy). His place of exile is now the site of **Kalaupapa National Historical Park**★★ *(see p160)* reachable by foot, small plane or mule.
In more recent years, the island was a sleepy community of ranches and pineapple plantations. Since the Del Monte® plantation closed in the early 1980s, tourism has become an economic necessity, but it's extremely low-key. Downtown is a mere two blocks long. You can still buy a burger for less than three bucks at the Molokai Drive-In! This island is all about wide-open spaces, where mountains meet ocean. You want nightclubs? Go to Maui!

Hawaii Tourism Authority/Ron Dahlquist

Sunset at Molokai

Touring Tip
Check out the cool kayak trips offered by Molokai Fish and Dive (departs from Kaunakakai Wharf) and Molokai Outdoors (at mile marker 16 on the East End).

The downside to Molokai (or the upside, depending on your point of view) is that there's not much in the way of posh restaurants, boutiques or nightclubs. You'll be clued in to that fact when you arrive: a popular T-shirt reads, "Molokai Night Life."

Fast Facts
- Molokai measures 38 miles long and 10 miles wide.
- The world's tallest ocean cliffs loom above Molokai's north shore.
- Molokai is home to 8,000 residents and the state's highest percentage of native Hawaiians (60%).
- The island, site of a leper colony from 1866 to 1969, was long shunned by visitors.

BEACHES

Papohaku Beach hosts dancers and musicians from all over the state for the Ka Hula Piko Festival (third weekend in May). Rock on, Molokai!

Murphy's Beach ★

Mile marker 20, Kamehameha Hwy. (Rte. 450), in eastern Molokai. Parking on the south side of the highway, just beyond mile marker. No restrooms or showers on-site.

Murphy's Beach, or 20 Mile Beach as it's also known, makes an excellent snorkeling spot, thanks to the barrier reef that runs alongside it. Enjoy great views of Maui and Lanai from a choice spot on the tawny sand. Just beyond the beach is a fish pond. Murphy's Beach makes a great stop if you're driving East End Drive *(Kamehameha V Highway)*, especially if you stopped for snacks along the way (there are no eats here, or nearby). Heading east, stop at Mana'e Goods and Grindz for cold drinks, sandwiches, and interesting bagged snacks like dried shrimp and hot (as in spicy) cuttlefish!

Papohaku Beach

Kaluakoi Rd., 5mi northwest of Maunaloa, western Molokai. The beach has three access points from Kaluakoi Rd.; all are marked with signs.

Nearly three miles long, and up to 60 yards wide, Papohaku has more surface area than any other beach in the islands.
This broad, gorgeous stretch of beige-colored sand is backed by dunes and lapped by turquoise waters—wonderful for sunbathing but not good for swimming or snorkeling, since riptides and rogue surf threaten. The beach has restrooms, picnic tables, and campsites.

Dixie Maru Beach ★

Off Kaluakoi Rd., northwest of Maunaloa, western Molokai. Take Kaluakoi Rd. to Papohaku Rd.; 5mi past Papohuku Beach Park, turn right.

Named after a shipwreck, this lovely scoop of bronze sand is the only swimmable beach on Molokai. There are no facilities here, just water and sand, bordered by lava rock and a fringe of shade trees. It takes some driving to get here—and most beachgoers get no farther than Papohaku Beach—so it never gets crowded (but then, what does on Molokai?).

Hula, Anyone?

According to ancient legend, the goddess Laka first danced the hula on a hill in Molokai, thus making the island the birthplace of the hula. This certainly seems plausible in May, when the **Ka Hula Piko Festival** brings scores of hula groups and musicians from the other islands.

Held on the shores of Papohaku Beach Park, the festival, whose name translates to "Center of the Dance," celebrates the different forms of traditional hula, accompanied by arts and crafts exhibits, Hawaiian games and music.
For schedules and information, call 808-552-2800 or check online at www.molokaievents.com.

MUST SEE MOLOKAI

NATURAL SITES

Papohaku Beach hosts dancers and musicians from all over the state for the Ka Hula Piko Festival (third weekend in May). Rock on, Molokai!

Moomomi Dunes★

Hwy 480, 3mi past Hoolehua town. 808-553-5236.

Set on the northwest coast of the island, this wild and windswept landscape is managed by the Nature Conservancy of Hawaii. The 921-acre property is a haven for wildlife watchers looking for native shorebirds like sanderlings and golden plovers, and the colony of endangered Hawaiian monk seals—often spotted sunbathing on the golden-sand beach. The Nature Conservancy runs monthly guided hikes here, but perhaps the best way to enjoy this pristine area is simply to roam, explore, and take in the vastness of the raging ocean and salt-splashed dunes.

SCENIC DRIVES

The southeast shore has stunning views. And, Molokaians point out, you can watch the sun rise and set from the same spot!

East End Drive (Kamehameha V Highway)★★

Hwy. 450, along the southeastern and eastern shoreline, from Kaunakakai east to Halawa. 27mi one way (allow a half-day for round-trip).

This spectacular drive skirts Molokai's mountains on one side and the Pacific Ocean on the other. Heading east from Kaunakakai, you'll quickly reach Kakahaia Beach Park, a national wildlife refuge that's a haven for local birds. At mile marker 10, look for St. Joseph's Catholic Church, built by Father Damien in 1876 and marked by a statue of the famous priest. Big tumbles of black lava rock are scattered along the winding, one-lane road, which gets really gorgeous after mile marker 20 or so. If you have yet to see the endangered nene (Hawaiian goose, *see p62*),

Halawa Valley

Hawaii Tourism Authority/Ron Dahlquist

you're likely to see them crossing the road here—near mile marker 23—there's even a sign that says "nene crossing."

The road heads inland, and you'll pass through a stand of long-needled Australian pines. After a series of wild twists and hill climbs, the road emerges at Halawa Valley, Molokai's most breathtaking spot, set off by velvety green hillsides and sparkling waterfalls.

159

HISTORIC SITES

About 76,000 visitors each year visit one of the country's most poignant but beautiful spots, the leper colony of Kalaupapa.

Kalaupapa National Historical Park★★

Access is by Molokai Air Shuttle (800-428-1231), foot, or mule ride (808-567-7550; www.muleride.com; $175/person; includes park tour and lunch). A steep 3.2mi trail with 26 switchbacks begins at Palaau State Park (Rte. 470, 10mi north of Kaunakakai). There is no road access between Kalaupapa and the rest of Molokai. 808-567-6802. www.nps.gov/kala. Park open Mon–Sat by tour only (Damien Tours, $40; no tours Sun or 16th of month). Ages 16 and up.

This unique site encompasses a 13.6-square-mile peninsula separated from the rest of Molokai by a 1,700-foot cliff. Victims of Hansen's Disease (leprosy) were relocated to this beautiful windswept promontory in 1866. In 1873 Father Damien de Veuster, a Belgian priest, arrived to live and work (and die, in 1889) among the infected. His original St. Philomena's Roman Catholic Church stands above the ruins of the village of Kalawao. Two dozen elderly leprosy patients, who pose no health threat to adult visitors, continue to live here.

Halawa Valley Falls & Cultural Hike

Contact Molokai Fish & Dive, 808-553-5926. www.molokaifishanddive.com. Tours last four hours; hiking distance is 4.5mi. Wear a swimsuit under your clothes and good hiking shoes. Bring water, lunch, and (definitely!) insect repellent. $35.

The site of the first Hawaiian settlement on Molokai, the Halawa Valley is steeped in history and legend. With native guide Lawrence Aki, you'll hike past ancient *loʻi* (taro patches), taste wild apples, see the ruins of ancient temples and fertility sites, and view two magnificent waterfalls, Moolua and Hipuapua. Try swimming in the cool, deep pools of 250ft Mooula Falls.

Halawa Falls

© Mike Brake/Bigstockphoto.com

FOR FUN

Having a good time on Molokai isn't about visiting tourist attractions, it's all about soaking up the raw beauty and laid-back vibe.

Purdy's Macadamnia Nut Farm

Hawaiianweb.com © Cassandra Dieterle

Purdy's Macadamia Nut Farm ★

Lihi Pali Ave., Kualapuu. 808-567-6001. http://molokai-aloha.com/macnuts. Open year-round Tue–Fri 9:30am–3:30pm, Sat 10am–2pm, weather permitting.

You'll stop simply to buy a bag of home-roasted macadamia nuts, but you'll find yourself admiring the five-acre orchard, and end up with a hammer in your hand, cracking open some nuts with a member of the Purdy family.

Aloha Friday Sunset Celebration

Hula Shores, Hotel Molokai, Kamehameha V Hwy., Kaunakakai. 8080553-5347. www.hotelmolokai.com.

It'll take you just a few minutes to make new friends at the open-air hotel bar (one of only two bars on the island where draft beer is sold), but if it's Friday night, you won't have much time to chat. Once the tiki torches are lit, the band sets up, the music begins, and the

Molokai Hoe Canoe Race

Considered Molokai's biggest annual social and athletic event, the 41-mile race across the treacherous waters of the Kaiwi Channel to Oahu ranks as the world championship of long-distance outrigger-canoe racing. The contest, held in October, starts at the rocky harbor of Hale o Lono, on the southwest coast of Molokai, and ends at Duke Kahanamoku Beach in Waikiki. What began as an inter-island race with three teams in 1952, has mushroomed into a popular event that lures as many as 100 teams of racers from around the world each year. *For more information, call 808-259-7112 or visit www.holoholo.org.*

Hawaiianweb.com © Cassandra Dieterle

party has officially begun! This is the place for nightlife on Molokai, and Friday night is the most happening night of the week!

Hike Kamakou Preserve

In east central Molokai. Maps and directions are available from the Nature Conservancy office at 23 Pueo Pl. (off Hwy 460, 3mi west of Kaunakakai). 808-553-5236. www.nature.org/hawaii. Open year-round Mon–Fri 7:30am–3pm. Best months to visit are Aug and Sept.

The jewel of Molokai is the 2,774-acre Kamakou Preserve, home to more than 250 species of Hawaiian plants, at least 219 of which are found no place else in the world. The peak of the preserve, about 5,000 feet above sea level, is the highest point on the island. This beautiful plot of land was donated by Molokai Ranch to the Nature Conservancy. The conservancy runs monthly guided hikes through the rain forest *(call or*

Will You Ferry Me?
Want to ferry from Maui to Molokai? The *Molokai Princess* (866-307-6524; www.molokaiferry.com) offers service (a 90min trip) between Lahaina and Kaunakakai Harbor, departing from Lahaina Harbor on Maui *(at 7:15am and 6pm Mon–Sat)*.
You can spend the day exploring Molokai and return to Maui in late afternoon—just in time for dinner at the oceanfront **Hula Grill**, north of Lahaina in Kaanapali *(see p173)*.

check online for schedule), providing transportation to trailheads from their office. If you do it yourself, you'll need a four-wheel-drive vehicle just to reach the preserve, and then you'll park and walk from the entrance to **Waikolu Lookout** (the main trailhead). August and September, the driest months, are the best time to visit, since it's notoriously easy to get stuck in the mud around here.

Waikolu means "three waters" in Hawaiian, and you'll quickly figure out why: waterfalls are everywhere. The elevation at the lookout is 3,700 feet, although rain and clouds often affect visibility. Check in with the Nature Conservancy before you go, so you'll be updated on trail conditions; routes are well-marked with some boardwalks.

The main trail in the preserve is Pepeopae Trail, which begins about three miles past the Waikolu Lookout. On this path, you'll traverse a lovely bog and lush vegetation, and end up at **Pelekunu Valley Overlook**.

Kamakou Preserve

Hawaiianweb.com © Cassandra Dieterle

MOLOKAI

MUST DO

KAHOOLAWE AND NIIHAU

At present, these islands are off-limits to visitors without an invitation.
See map on inside front cover.

Kahoolawe

The island of Kahoolawe, smallest of Hawaii's eight major islands and part of Maui County, has a colorful past. It has served as a penal colony for Catholics, then a ranch, then it was a base for US Army military exercises. After the attack on Pearl Harbor in 1941, the US Navy took over, and began using it for bombing practice.

Nearly every instrument of war used by the US military and its allies since World War II has bombarded this island, where unexploded munitions still lurk on the beaches and in the offshore waters. The island was ultimately returned to Hawaii, with much fanfare and blowing of conch-shell horns, in 2003.

A $400 million clean-up plan was launched, and much of the island is now deemed safe for controlled visits, but access is strictly limited. The only people currently on the island are archeologists, volunteers restoring native habitat, and Hawaiians engaged in spiritual practices.

Niihau

Meanwhile, Kauai tourists hear whispers of Hawaii's "Forbidden Island," Niihau (pronounced *Nee-ee-how*). Set 17 miles off the

> **Touring Tip**
> For the lowdown on tours and hunting safaris to the privately owned "Forbidden Island" of Niihau, as well as other island information, call the **Niihau Helicopters** office *(808-877-441-3500; www.niihau.us/heli.html)*.

west coast of Kauai, this privately owned 72-square-mile island has no paved roads and no electricity. The 160 or so inhabitants are mostly native islanders who live a traditional Hawaiian lifestyle.

Also at home on the coast of Niihau are monk seals, In fact, the largest colony in the major Hawaiian Islands lives here.

Niihau was once a ranching outpost. Now this arid island stays afloat financially by serving as a base for support services for NASA and the US Navy, and by operating helicopter tours and hunting safaris (Polynesian boar, feral sheep, and, on a limited basis, Barbary sheep, eland and oryx antelope).

Curious about the island? For a price ($365 per person), **Niihau Helicopters** *(see box, above)* offers half-day trips to Niihau. After an aerial tour, you'll land on a secluded beach for swimming and beachcombing.

> **A Wealth of Shells**
> Niihau is famous for its beautifully intricate shell leis. Local kahelelani shells are fashioned into exquisite pieces, which can fetch thousands of dollars. A Niihau shell lei is displayed in the British Museum (London, UK) as a memento of Captain Cook's first visit to the Hawaiian Islands.

Hawaiian Culture

About 19 percent of Hawaii's population call themselves Hawaiian, although the number with pure Hawaiian blood may be less than one percent—perhaps about 10,000. Many Hawaiians died in the 19th century from diseases introduced by European settlers. Over the past 150 years, native islanders intermarried easily, especially with Caucasians (*haoles* in Hawaiian) and Chinese. But the natives' influence on local culture goes far beyond their numbers: Some of the best-known aspects of Hawaiian culture—music, dance, food and the welcoming aloha attitude—have been absorbed by all those who live in Hawaii.

For at least 1,000 years, the Polynesian Hawaiians lived alone in the islands. They came in great double-hulled canoes—first from the Marquesas Islands between AD 500 and 750, later from Tahiti about 1100—and built houses of thatched grass. Their lives revolved around fishing, cultivating taro (a starchy edible root) and yams, gathering fruit and raising pigs. With their sophisticated knowledge of astronomy, the early peoples calculated the effect of the seasons on farming and harvesting. They imbued birds, fish and inanimate objects with supernatural powers; things that were sacred were labeled as *kapu*, or forbidden.

As the centuries passed, stories of their former lands became mere songs and lore.

Language: Hawaiians retained the basic spoken Polynesian language, adapting it to their own needs. After 1820, American missionaries transliterated Hawaiian to make it a written language, reducing the number of consonants to just seven—h, k, l, m, n, p and w. The Hawaiian language today is regularly spoken in daily life only on the private island of Niihau. Hawaiian locals speak either standard English or a type of pidgin composed mainly of English words, but with unusual inflections and numerous Chinese, Japanese and Filipino words stirred into the conversation.

Playing guitar: Many other cultural aspects were developed after contact with the West. From Spanish-speaking cowboys (*paniolo*) on the Big Island, Hawaiians learned guitar; they loosened the strings to change the tuning and invented the "slack-key" style of playing.

Music: When Portuguese immigrants arrived in the late 19th century, Hawaiians learned to play the four-stringed *braga*, renaming it the **ukulele**.

This instrument, along with a drum, was played to accompany the hula. Originally performed only by men as part of an ancient religious ritual, hula evolved into a graceful dance for women. Grass skirts were a 20th century import from Micronesia; dancers were traditionally clad in ti leaves.

RESTAURANTS: BIG ISLAND

The venues listed below were selected for their ambience, location and/or value for money. Rates indicate the average cost of an appetizer, an entrée and a dessert for one person (not including tax, gratuity or beverages). Most restaurants are open daily (except where noted) and accept major credit cards. Call for information regarding reservations, dress code and opening hours.

Luxury	$$$$	Over $75	Inexpensive	$$	$25–$50
Expensive	$$$	$50–$75	Budget	$	Under $25

BIG ISLAND

Hualailai Grille

$$$$ Asian
Four Seasons Hualailai Hotel, 100 Kaupulehu Dr., Kailua-Kona. 808-325-8525. www.hualalai resort.com.

Huggo's

If you're a fan of chef Alan Wong's Honolulu outpost, you won't be disappointed here. Diners use words like "sublime" and "exquisite" to describe Wong's culinary artistry. From creative cocktails like lychee martinis to steamed opakapak with shrimp and pork hash, dinner feels like a celebration here. (Can't decide? Try the seven-course tasting menu.) The crowning touch is the irresistible vanilla bean cheesecake with caramel sauce and Kona coffee ice cream.

Donatoni's

$$$ Italian
At the Hilton Waikoloa Village Resort, 425 Waikoloa Beach Dr., Waikoloa. 808-886-1234. www. hiltonwaikoloavillage.com. Dinner only.

To get the full romantic effect of Donatoni's, cruise to the restaurant by boat from the hotel lobby.

Once there, you'll dine on a garden terrace with ocean views, on seductive dishes like shrimp and scallops nestled in pasta with a to-die-for cream sauce, or fusilli with artichokes and pancetta.

Huggo's

$$$ Seafood
75-5828 Kahakai Rd., Kailua-Kona. 808-329-1493. www.huggos.com.

This place is a local institution, complete with sherbet-hued sunsets and technicolor cocktails that only enhance the food—think seared ahi, pasta with vegetables and wild mushrooms, and chicken cooked in ti leaves. The thatched bar, Huggo's on the Rocks, is an island hot spot for noshing on *pupu* (appetizers) and dancing at the water's edge.

Kilauea Lodge

Merriman's

$$$ Hawaiian Regional
Kawaihae Rd., Opelu Plaza,
Waimea. 808-885-6822.
www.merrimanshawaii.com.

Owner Peter Merriman is one of
Hawaii's superstar chefs, and a real
master at creating cutting-edge
dishes out of fresh local ingredi-
ents. Lamb comes from nearby
Kahua Ranch, and it's roasted with
plum sauce and served with
papaya-mint relish. Wok-charred
ahi is a signature dish, as is
Merriman's Caesar salad, to which
he adds sashimi, Pahoa corn and
shrimp fritters.

Hilo Bay Café

$$ American
315 Makaala St. #109., Hilo.
808-935-4939. www.hilobaycafe.
com. Lunch and dinner.

Inauspiciously located in a strip
mall near Wal-Mart, this small
storefront restaurant wins fans
with vibrantly flavored dishes that
often incorporate local ingredients.
Regulars suggest that standard
menu items hit the mark more
often than daily specials.
Among the dishes winning raves

are the ahi poke, spinach salad
with strawberries and candied
macadamia nuts, and the catch
of the day, served with a kick of
wasabi sauce. For dessert, try
blueberry bread pudding, a fresh
alternative to the ubiquitous lava
cake. Service is casual and friendly.

Kilauea Lodge Restaurant

$$ Continental
Old Volcano Rd.,
Volcano Village. 808-967-7366.
www.kilaualodge.com.

Cozy, rustic Kilauea Lodge is an
inviting stop on a cool night in
Volcano, especially when there are
logs crackling in the fireplace. This
is the fine-dining option near Ki-
lauea volcano, with classic entrées
featuring game (antelope flambé)
and *hasenpfeffer* (rabbit braised in
wine), along with vegetarian offer-
ings and great soups.

Quinn's Almost by the Sea

$$ Seafood
75–5655 Palani Rd., Kailua-Kona.
808-329-3822. Lunch and dinner.

This small, older restaurant gets
eclipsed by some of the fancier
places in town, but in-the-know

local folk consider it the go-to destination for good seafood (and great value). The ono fish and chips wins raves by all (even finicky kids and non-fish-lovers), so you might not get around to trying the tasty prawns. Shame! Quinn's onion rings are "totally awesome," according to afficianados of the deep-fried delicacy. Ask for a seat on the patio.

Island Lava Java

$ American

75-5799 Alii Dr., Alii Sunset Plaza, Kailua-Kona. 808-327-2161. www.islandlavajavakona.com. Dinner only.

This cute little waterfront coffee-house is a real find. The menu features grass-fed beef, local organic goat cheese, and house-baked breads and desserts. Nice touch: plates are garnished with purple orchids. For breakfast, you can't go wrong with banana-mac-nut pancakes with coconut syrup, and it's always a good time for kalua pork tacos with garlic mashed potatoes and green salad with tangy homemade vinaigrette.

Ken's House of Pancakes

$ American
1730 Kamehameha Ave., Hilo. 808-935-8711.

"K-Hop," as the locals call it, is an old-fashioned coffee shop, featuring live and onions, French toast, hash, and, of course, perfectly golden pancakes—all served with a side order of local color. Favorites include shredded kalua pig on a hoagie, French toast made with sweet Portuguese bread, and coconut custard pie. Come Sunday for "all-you-can-eat" spaghetti night.

Tex's Drive In

$ International

On Hwy. 19, Honokaa. 808-775-0598. Also in Pahala. http://dutchhawaii.com/ default.aspx.

The major attraction at Tex's is a Portuguese specialty called mala-sadas, best described as a gourmet donut hole. Rolled in sugar, these sweet treats ooze gooey stuff like pineapple-papaya preserves. These make a terrific breakfast, as the bevy of early-bird regulars will attest. The rest of the menu is an eclectic mix, ranging from basic burgers to Korean chicken. Try the homemade sweet-potato chips.

What's Shakin'

$ Health Food
27-999 Old Mamalahoa Hwy., Pepeekeo. 808-964-3080. No dinner.

Set along scenic Pepeekeo Drive *(see p36)*, this unassuming wooden house is a must-stop, if just for a fresh-fruit smoothie. These are among the best you'll ever taste, featuring delectable blends of fruits from the owner's farm. Try the Papaya Paradise, with pineapple, papaya, banana and coconut. Lunch items rely on organic local ingredients. Try the Blue Hawaii, a blue-corn tamale with homemade salsa, served with a crunchy green salad topped with sesame dressing.

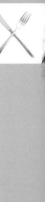

RESTAURANTS: BIG ISLAND

MAUI

Mama's Fish House

$$$ Seafood
*799 Poho Pl., 1.5mi east of Paia.
808-579-8488. www.mamasfish
house.com.*

If you want to treat yourself to
Maui's best tables, put this one
on your list. You can't beat the
ambience: Mama's is a wonderful
converted beach house, awash in
palm trees and Polynesian décor.
Tables are adorned in tapas-print
cloths, a lively backdrop for fresh
fish dishes that look like art on
a plate—and taste heavenly.
Stand-out dishes include Tahitian
poisson cru, an appetizer of ono
(a local fish) marinated in lime and
coconut milk. Selections of fresh
island fish always include at least
four different preparations. Ask for
the chocolate mousse "pearl," in a
tuille cookie shell.

Island Bouillabaise and Crispy
Moi, Mama's Fish House

© Tony Novak-Clifford/Mama's Fish House

Nick's Fishmarket Maui

$$$ Seafood
*Fairmont Kea Lani Hotel,
4100 Wailea Alanui. 808-879-7224.
www.tristarrestaurants.com.
Dinner only.*

Nick's Fish Market

Nick's Fish Market

The service here is absolutely
impeccable—you'll be served by
a team of three people who will
refill your water glass every three
seconds (or so it seems). All of this
would seem like so much postur-
ing, except that the food is simply
exquisite. Fresh fish and lobster
are perfectly prepared and artfully
presented; the lamb melts in your
mouth. The room is lovely, too,
perched above the pool with stars
overhead; stylish art-glass lighting
adds a warm amber glow.

I 'O

$$$ Pacific Rim
*505 Front St., Lahaina.
808-661-8422. www.iomaui.com.
Lunch and dinner only.*

You might catch the sounds of
Hawaiian music from the luau
show next door. Otherwise, you'll
notice the "oohs" and "ahhs" of
happy diners feasting on chef
James McDonald's inventive

"Contemporary Pacific" cuisine. His Thai curry asparagus soup (topped with Maine lobster and tarragon) was featured in *Bon Appetit*; guests rave about the crab cakes and the crispy ahi—a winning combination of rare sashimi tuna with a nori-panko crust served with green papaya salad and a ginger-soy vinaigrette. Like the food, the room is sleek, contemporary, and very tasteful. Cool to a fault, I'O is the antithesis of a rowdy, two-for-one-beers tourist trap.

Hula Grill

$$ Hawaiian Regional
Whalers Village, 2435 Kaanapali Pkwy., Kaanapali. 808-667-6636. www.hulagrill.com.

Chef Peter Merriman divides his time between Hula Grill and Merriman's on the Big Island, and it's clear he has another hit on his hands. Set on the beach, with live hula (of course!), the Hula Grill has a great vibe, and the signature Merriman touch with seafood. Fresh fish is grilled on wood or paired with a choice of sauces and salsas, and some of the smallest dishes make the biggest splash (crab-macadamia-nut wontons, anyone?). Save room for the gourmet ice cream sandwich, with creamy vanilla stuffed between giant chunks of chocolate-mac-adamia-nut brownies.

Great Cheap Eats in Maui
Eskimo Candy, at 2665 Wai Wai Pl, Kihei, is a great little hole-in-the-wall for fried fish and ahi poke. Whaler's General Store (located in the Shops at Wailea mall) makes a handy stop for meals on the go—deli sandwiches, muffins, salads.

Anthony's Coffee Co.

$ American
90 Hana Hwy., Paia. No dinner. 808-579-8340 or 800-882-6509. www.anthonyscoffee.com.

Breakfast and lunch are the way to go here. Anthony's roasts its own coffee, and sells it by the pound and by the cup, including pure Kona and their own special blends. For a hearty way to start your day, try Kalua Pork Benedict or the breakfast wrap (eggs, tomato, cheese, rice, bacon); you'll want to go lighter if you can't resist a pineapple-coconut muffin (and you shouldn't!). Anthony's makes an fantastic picnic lunch, too, with hefty sandwiches that don't fall apart, served with a side salad, if you choose. You'll note the sign which says, "Shirts and shoes please," but bikini tops and bare chests rule!

Jawz Fish Tacos

$ Mexican
Across the street from Makena Beach, Makena. 808-874-8226.

The original Jawz was, and still is, a wood-shingled taco truck, parked across from Makena Beach. They make wonderful fish tacos and terrific smoothies. Jawz Fish Tacos Island Style Grill *(1279 S. Kihei Rd., in the Azeka Mauka Shopping Center, Kihei; 808-874-8226)* offers the same great tacos, burritos and salads, plus Maui's largest salsa bar. Top your taco with roasted habanero-pepper salsa, made with pineapple and carrots. Now that's salsa!

RESTAURANTS: BIG ISLAND

KAUAI

Café Hanalei

$$$ Pacific Rim
5520 Ka Haku Rd., Princeville. 808-826-9644. www.princeville.com.

Dining at this intimate open-air, terraced space at the elegant Princeville resort *(see p182)*, overlooking the stunning Hanalei Bay, Bali Hai and the shimmering waters of the Pacific Ocean, is one of the most romantic dining experiences on Kauai. Combine it with innovative, expertly prepared food, and you have a meal you won't soon forget. Signature dishes on the often-changing menu include the macadamia nut crusted swordfish and pan seared ahi loin.

Tidepools

$$$ Hawaiian
1571 Poipu Bay, Grand Hyatt Kauai, Koloa. 808-240-6456. www.kauai.hyatt.com. Dinner only. Reservations recommended.

Love is in the air at this open-air, thatched-roof dining room, suspended over exotic koi ponds and cascading waterfalls. Gas-lit lanterns twinkle in the surrounding tropical gardens and candles flicker as diners feast on appetizers

Tidepools

like pancetta wrapped sea scallops or jumbo crab cakes. Follow up with entrées like garlic chili glazed opah with macadamia nut rice or grilled huli huli chicken breast with Okinawan sweet potato purée.

Gaylord's

$$ Hawaiian
2087 Kaumua\lii Hwy., Lihue. 808-245-9593. www.gaylords kauai.com.

Gaylord's

This gracious, open-air dining room, overlooking 35 acres of gardens and fields, was once a 1930s plantation home. Since 1986, the Wallace family has been serving Kauai islanders and visitors plates of fresh fish, top-quality steaks and traditional Hawaiian fare. Relax in wicker chairs, bumped up to white-linen-draped tables, and order hoisin braised spring rolls, slow-roasted prime rib or the fire-grilled ahi. They also host traditional Hawaiian luaus.

Kintaro's

$$ Japanese
4-370 Kuhio Hwy. (Rte. 56), Wailua. 808-822-3341. Closed Mon.

Quite simply, this no-frills restaurant is the best place for sushi on the island. Its large, cavernous dining rooms are nearly always full with loyal locals and savvy visitors. Service is fast, friendly and efficient; the sushi is wonderfully fresh. There are full plates of Japanese entrées but most folks make a meal of their favorite sushi and dim sum offerings. Chefs perform at some tables, slicing, dicing and cooking meats and vegetables tableside.

Roy's Poipu Bar& Grill

$$ Hawaiian
2360 Kiahuna Plantation Dr., Poipu. 808-742-5000. www.roys restaurant.com. Dinner only.

Renowned Chef Roy Yamaguchi brings his signature—and award-winning—Hawaiian fusion cuisine to this sleek dining room in the Poipu Shopping Center. Start with Roy's Canoe Appetizer, with shrimp sticks, Szechuan baby back ribs, island ahi poke, pork and shrimp lumpia, and crisped seafood potstickers You'll find all his favorite entrees here, too, like the opakapaka smothered in macadamia-nut sauce, blackened ahi with spicy mustard butter, yellowfin ahi poketini, and hibachi salmon. Despite the proliferation of Roy's restaurants across the country, this place still draws crowds and raves.

Roy's Poipu Bar&Grill

Roy's Restaurant

$ American
2360 Kiahuna, in Poipu Shopping Village, Koloa. 808-742-1979. www.ebseatshawaii.com. No dinner.

If you're looking for a quick bite to eat, you can't beat this casual, open-air restaurant. Fresh ingredients and creative combinations, along with value-packed prices, make this small eatery one of Kauai's favorites. Local residents and visitors alike come for tasty breakfast sandwiches and egg dishes (try Harry's Hawaiian Style Fried Rice Omelet) and lunch items, like the roasted veggie and goat cheese sandwich or wild mushroom meatloaf.

Ono Family Restaurant

$ American
4-1292 Kuhio Hwy., Kapaa. 808-822-1710. No dinner.

What's not to like about a place that serves meatloaf and eggs for breakfast? This family-owned, longtime island favorite is a great place for casual eats.
You'll find more than 15 omelet choices and a variety of special egg dishes, along with hotcakes (try the macadamia nut) and specialty coffees and fruit smoothies. For lunch, there's a massive lineup of sandwiches and burgers, plus Oriental stir-frys, Portuguese-style pork platters, and fish and chips—all at prices that won't bust the budget.

RESTAURANTS: KAUAI

OAHU

Chef Mavro

$$$$ French

1969 S. King St., Honolulu. 808-944-4714. www.chefmavro.com. Dinner only.

One of the finest restaurants on Oahu, Chef Mavro serves up unique fusion dishes, combining French haute cuisine with fresh Hawaiian ingredients. Owner-chef George Mavrothalassitis, a native of southern France, has won acclaim for his tasting menus that pair each item with wine Poached rock fish soup with aioli sauce, grilled hamakua mushroom and macaroni gratin, filet mignon and corned short ribs, and roasted pork loin with cannellini bean purée are some of the dishes you may find on the ever-changing menu.

La Mer

$$$$ French

2199 Kalia Rd., in the Halekulani Hotel, Honolulu. 808-923-2311. www.halekulani.com. Dinner only.

Itching to dress up? Want to splurge? This formal restaurant offers the best in haute cuisine. The food, combining French techniques with fresh Hawaiian ingredients, matches the spectacular setting overlooking Waikiki beach. Chef Yves Garnier offers up creative twists on classics, like the crispy skin onago fillet on a warm potato terrine, roasted goose breast with lavender honey, Chilean sea bass and pork belly, medallions of milk-fed veal and sliced tournedos of Japanese Wagyubeef.

Alan Wong's Restaurant

$$$ Hawaiian Regional

1857 S. King St., 3rd floor, Honolulu. 808-949-2526. www.alanwongs.com. Dinner only.

Arguably the best restaurant in Hawaii, Alan Wong's continues to rack up well-deserved accolades. The dining room's design is clean, crisp and inviting, with neutral walls, white tablecloths and an open kitchen. Start with appetizers like crispy won ton ahi poke balls with wasabi sauce or seafood cakes. For entrées, try the ginger crusted onaga or the olive oil poached lamb rib eye served with a taro hash cake.

Chai's Island Bistro

$$$ Pacific Rim

Aloha Tower Marketplace, Pier 9, Honolulu. 808-585-0011. www.chaisislandbistro.com.

Chef Chai Chaowasaree has built a loyal following, who crave his innovative Pacific-Rim cuisine. This relaxed, energetic eatery, with indoor and outdoor seating and live entertainment, offers a variety of creative dishes made with fresh local ingredients. Start with the eggplant and zucchini soufflé or salmon tartar. For entrées, you'll find a wide selection that changes seasonally. Try the Pacific Rim

La Mer

Halekulani Hotel

ciopino in coconut broth or the wok-seared jumbo prawns with spicy chili ginger sauce.

Duke's Waikiki

$$ Hawaiian
2335 Kalakaua Ave., Honolulu. 808-922-2268. www.dukeswaikiki.com.

Duke's Waikiki

Duke's Waikiki

You won't go away hungry at this restaurant, named after Duke Kahanamoku, the father of surfing. Known for its hefty steak and fresh seafood dishes and lively bar *(see p141)*, the place is always bustling. The dining room is beach-bar casual—it sits on Waikiki Beach with great ocean views—and is filled with surfing memorabilia. Pupu includes spicy sugarcane shrimp or macadamia-nut and crab won tons. Then it's on to prime steaks, mango-glazed barbecue ribs, and fresh fish dishes, each offered with a variety of preparations and sauces. All dinners come with the legendary Duke's salad bar.

Hula Grill

$$ Hawaiian
At the Outrigger Waikiki, 2335 Kalakaua Ave., Honolulu. 808-923-4852. www.hulagrill waikiki.com. No lunch.

This elegantly casual beachfront eatery at the Outrigger Waikiki on the Beach resort is popular with locals and visitors alike for its tasty but simpl;y prepared fresh fish dishes and melt-in-your-mouth steaks. Try the rice paper poke rolls or the crab and macadamia nut wontons, before moving on to the Tandoori-style opah or traditional standbys like BBQ ribs, steaks, and stir-frys.

Indigo

$$ Asian
1121 Nuuanu Ave., Honolulu. Closed Sun & Mon. 808-521-2900. www.indigo-hawaii.com. Closed Sun, Mon.

Owner-chef Glenn Chu, raised in the Manoa Valley, has designed an eclectic menu that consistently earns Honolulu's best dining awards. The warmly decorated dining room, near old Chinatown, features Indonesian hand-carved wood paneling, Chinese lanterns, tropical plants and bamboo accents. You'll have a tough time narrowing down your choice from a menu that may include tempura ahi rolls, Hanoi shrimp and enoki mushroom summer rolls, seafood coconut curry soup, and entrees like the Pacific fish in banana leaf with cocoa bean curry and the miso-marinated salmon filet.

Keo's in Waikiki

$$ Thai
2028 Kuhio Ave., Honolulu. 808-951-9355. www.keosthaicuisine.com.

As Hawaii's preeminent Thai chef, Keo Sananikone has done much to help popularize Thai cuisine in America. Of his five local restaurants, this is nearest to major hotels. The extensive menu

173

lists starters like crispy noodles, summer rolls, and papaya salad; main courses include curry dishes, seafood selections (try the Indonesian shrimp in peanut sauce or the crispy mahi-mahi) and house specialties like grilled country game hen or Bangkok duck.

Roy's Restaurant

$$ **Hawaiian**
6600 Kalanianaole Hwy., Honolulu. 808-396-7697. www.roysrestaurant.com.

Roy's Restaurant

Roy's Restaurant

Renowned Chef Roy Yamaguchi and his talented staff fire up dishes like opakapaka smothered in macadamia-nut sauce, roasted duck with passion fruit, blackened ahi, wood-grilled Szechuan-spiced ribs, hibachi salmon and more. The first of Roy's more than 30 restaurants around the world, this two-level dining room, with its open kitchen and casual vibe, overlooks the Pacific Ocean.

Sam Choy's Diamond Head Restaurant

$$ **Hawaiian**
449 Kapahulu Ave., Honolulu. 808-732-8645. www.samchoy. com. Dinner & Sun brunch only.

Sam Choy's flagship restaurant is the setting for the popular local cooking show, Sam Choy's Kitchen, and a longtime local favorite. The best-selling cookbook author draws crowds of locals and visitors alike. The restaurant is friendly and unpretentious, and the servings are large.

The extensive selection of Choy classics includes Portuguese sausage-crusted mahimahi, red wine-braised short ribs and Sam's signature spiced, oven roasted duck.

Sansei Seafood Restaurant & Sushi Bar

$$ **Japanese**
Queens' Marketplace, Waikiki Beach Marriott Resort, Waikiki. 808-931-6286. www. sanseihawaii.com. Closed Sun.

If you're looking for fresh, creatively prepared seafood and sushi, you'll find it at this lively eatery, tucked in the popular Waikiki Beach Marriott Resort. Try the award-winning Japanese calamari salad, Asian shrimp cake, or mango-crab-salad roll. There are large plates, too, but most people —and rightfully so—come for the freshly prepared sushi.

Sansei Seafood Restaurant & Sushi Bar

Sansei Seafood Restaurant & Sushi Bar

Sushi Sasabune

$$ Japanese
1417 S. King St., Honolulu. Dinner only. 808-947-3800. Closed Sun.

Oh, my, my. Sushi lovers will think they have died and gone to heaven. This elegant little eatery takes its sushi very seriously (please use chopsticks so as not to squeeze the rice!) and the result is culinary art for the taste buds. Bites of the freshest finest fish, from California sea urchins to Boston halibut, Japanese yellowtail to Alaskan albacore—are nestled in warm rice, creating, arguably, the best sushi in Hawaii and beyond.

Giovanni's Shrimp Truck

$ Hawaiian
Truck is parked along Highway 83 between Turtle Bay and Kahuku.

There are plenty of shrimp trucks along the North Shore but this Oahu mainstay remains a favorite. The graffiti-covered white truck serves large platters of fresh-caught, shrimp with lemon and butter or hot and spicy (very hot!) sauces, and the not-to-be-beat scampi with chunks of garlic.

Hukilau Café

$ Hawaiian
55-662 Wahinepee St., Laie. 808-293-8616. No dinner. Closed Sun & Mon, and Sat lunch.

This down-to-earth restaurant is a must-stop for hungry locals. It's best known for its hefty breakfast platters, including faves like the beef stew omelette and homemade corned beef hash. Lunch plates are tasty, too; try the

mahimahi or shrimp tempura. Or, opt for the hefty Hukilua burger, a hamburger patty topped with teriyaki beef, fried egg, and grilled onions.

Ono Hawaiian Food

$ Hawaiian
726 Kapahulu Ave., Honolulu. 808-737-2275 for take-out. www.geocities.com/napavalley/ 9874. Closed Sun.

You can't beat this hole-in-the-wall eatery for traditional Hawaiian food. The local favorite for nearly 40 years, Onos is the place to go for luau-style kalua pig, steamed overnight in a wood-fired, underground oven. The signature laulau—ti-leaf-wrapped packets of taro leaves and chunks of pork—is another favorite. The heaping special plates come with big scoops of rice, poi, haupia, lomi lomi salmon and pipikaula.

Rainbow Drive-In

$ Hawaiian
3308 Kanaina Ave., Honolulu. 808-737-0177.

There are some things that inspire cravings. Such is the case for the Rainbow Diner's made-from-scratch chili. See for yourself, but don't stop with a mere bowl. Order up one of the classic mixed-plate lunches, too—a heaping dish of barbecued meat, fish, chicken or pork, piled high with scoops of the requisite macaroni salad and rice.

LANAI

Formal Dining Room at the Lodge at Koele

$$$$ **Contemporary American**

*1 Keamoku Dr., Lanai City.
808-565-3800 or 800-450-3704.
www.fourseasons.com/koele.
Dinner only.*

As the name implies, this top-end restaurant at the Lodge at Koele *(see p188)*, offers an elegant dining experience, noted for its high-quality cuisine and impeccable service. The stately dining room is bathed in soft light from flickering candles and a glowing log fire. On the menu you'll find well-executed classics, including steaks, lobster, fish and Hawaiian regional specialties—all at high prices.

Lanai City Grille

$$ **Hawaiian Fusion**

*828 Lanai Ave., at the Hotel Lanai,
Lanai City. 808-565-7211.
www.hotellanai.com. Dinner only.
Closed Mon & Tue.*

Formerly Henry Clay's Rotisserie, this warm and casual restaurant is now under the auspices of Beverly Gannon, one of the 12 original founders of the Hawaii Regional Cuisine movement.
The menu changes with the seasons and available ingredients, and includes fresh-caught local fish, poultry and beef dishes. Gannon has retained Henry Clay's popular, mouth-watering herb-marinated rotisserie chicken.

Pele's Other Garden

$ **American**

*Lanai City. 808-565-9628.
www.pelesothergarden.com.
Closed Sat & Sun.*

This tiny, bright bistro is the perfect place to stop for an overstuffed sandwich or burrito, organic salads, and homemade breads and soups. At night, order tasty, fresh-made pizzas and classic Italian dishes. The bistro has a full bar, too.

MOLOKAI

Kanemitsu Bakery & Restaurant

$ **Hawaiian**

*79 Ala Malama St., Kaunakakai.
808-553-5855. Closed Tue.*

This plain-Jane bakery is a great place to buy Molokai's distinctive sweet bread. Get it straight from the oven, to go, or nibble on it here, while you hang out with the regular breakfast crowd and catch the local scuttlebutt.

Kualapuu Cook House

$ **American**

*Hwy. 480, Kualapuu.
808-567-9655. Closed Mon morning and Sun.*

Be hungry. Be very hungry. This local, no-frills institution really shines come lunch time, when the kitchen sends out big plates of chicken, beef or pork stir-fry with eggs, rice, and macaroni salad. The grilled Mahi "burger" is a tasty choice. Things get fancier at dinner time, when they serve up great specials, like baby-back ribs in guava sauce.

HOTELS: BIG ISLAND

The properties listed below were selected for their ambience, location and/or value for money. Prices reflect the average cost for a standard double room for two people. Many hotels offer special discount packages; ask about them when you make your reservations. Price ranges quoted do not reflect the Hawaii hotel tax of 11.4%.

Luxury	**$$$$$**	Over $350	Inexpensive	**$$$**	$175–$250
Expensive	**$$$$**	$250–$350	Budget	**$$–$**	Under $175

BIG ISLAND

Four Seasons Hualalai

$$$$$ 243 rooms
100 Kaupulehu Dr., Kaupulehu-Kona. 808-325-8019 or 800-819-5053. www.fourseasons.com.

An intimate, bungalow-style resort on the water, this lush tropical retreat melts easily into the natural environment. Guests can swim in a saltwater pool (one of four ocean-front pools here) or cool off in outdoor rock showers after a round of golf or a spa treatment. Prefer a postcard-perfect, white-sand beach? Kukio and Kua Bay beaches are each a short drive away. Every room has its own private lanai and ocean views, along with all the luxurious touches you'd expect in a Four Seasons property. The gym (for those dedicated enough to work out on vacation) is large and well equipped. And did we mention the wonderful spa *(see p55)*? The caveat is that all this comes at a price. While the on-site restaurants are very good, they're pricey. And golfers can find more reasonable greens fees on the Waikoloa courses. But then again, this isn't the place to come if you're bargain-hunting, as the sprinkling of Hollywood types would attest.

Fairmont Orchid

$$$$ 540 rooms
One North Kaniku Dr., Kohala Coast. 808-885-2000 or 800-257-7544. www.fairmont.com.

Set on 32 acres of a sheltered lagoon, the Fairmont Orchid offers a hushed elegance. Guest rooms were refurbished in 2008 with a Hawaiian-style makeover, featuring island artwork, block-cut native wall coverings, and palm-leaf pillow shams. The Fairmont uses chemical-free cleansers and organic landscaping, and the resort's Spa Without Walls *(see p55)* offers outdoor massage. A children's program, water sports equipment rentals, and a bevy of restaurants round out the amenities.

Plush lobby of Four Seasons Hualalai

© Four Seasons

Hapuna Beach Prince Hotel

$$$$ 350 rooms
62-100 Kauna'oa Dr.,
Kohala Coast. 808-880-1111.
www.princeresortshawaii.com.

"This place isn't fancy, but it has a great vibe," according to happy guests who feel as if they've discovered a gem among Mauna Kea's resort hotels. Combine true Aloha Spirit (genuine friendliness) and gorgeous Hapuna Beach and you've got a winner here. Hawaiian plantation-style rooms are spacious, with private lanais. The open-air lobby is currently under renovation. A large free-form pool overlooks that amazing beach.

Hilton Waikoloa Village

$$$$ 1,240 rooms
425 Waikoloa Beach Dr.,
Waikoloa. 808-886-1234.
www.hiltonwaikoloavillage.com.

The Big Island's answer to Walt Disney World®, this waterfront resort whisks you to your room via monorail or boat. Seven million dollars' worth of artwork is displayed on the property, including a one-mile museum walkway. You can slide down a 175-foot waterslide, kayak in a lagoon, or swim with the dolphins.
Among the hotel's nine restaurants, Donatoni's *(see p165)* is the best bet.

Kona Village Resort

$$$$$ 125 rooms
Queen Kaahumanu Hwy., Kailua-Kona. 808-325-5555 or 800-367-5290. www.konavillage.com.

This Polynesian-style resort is a world unto itself. Hammocks

Kona Village Resort

sway beneath coconut palms beside thatched-roof beachfront cottages. Well-appointed hales, or houses, have no phones, televisions or radios to remind you of the outside world; if you don't want to be disturbed, just place a coconut outside your door. Kids and parents kayak and windsurf by day and enjoy luaus in the ocean-view restaurant by night.

Waikoloa Beach Marriott Resort

$$$ 555 rooms
69-275 Waikoloa Beach Dr.,
Waikoloa. 808-886-1234 or 888-924-5656. www.waikoloabeach marriott.com.

For an average room rate of less than $300 a night, this property offers loads of amenities, including a spa, children's activities and water

Kona Village Resort

Waikoloa Beach Marriott Resort

178

sports galore. The pool area is fabulous (there are six pools, plus ancient fish ponds), and the beach is even better—a luscious swath of crescent sand on Anaehoomalu Bay (aka A-Bay) on the Kohala Coast. On property, there's swimming, snorkeling, kayaking and windsurfing—anything else you want to do or see, they can arrange for you. Rooms are modern and clean, fine for a laid-back beach vacation. The on-site restaurant doesn't win rave reviews (although the buffet breakfast isn't bad), but there are plenty of other choices for dining in the 'hood.

Kilauea Lodge

$$ 14 rooms, 3 cottages
Old Volcano Rd., Volcano. 808-967-7366. www.kilauealodge.com.

Kilauea Lodge

Kilauea Lodge

Unless you're camping, this is your best bet for sleeping in the shadow of the Kilauea volcano (the lodge is located a mile from Hawaii Volcanoes National Park). Formerly a YMCA camp (c. 1938), this high-ceilinged, rustic lodge is a cozy, inviting place to stay on a cool night (and aren't they all, here?). Some rooms have gas fireplaces, and all are adorned with fresh flowers. Rates include a full breakfast. The on-property restaurant offers fine dining with an Old World, European flavor.

Waimea Gardens Cottage B&B

$$ 2 cottages
Off Mamalahoa Hwy, 2mi east of town, Waimea; 808-885-8550. www.waimeagardens.com. Three-night minimum stay.

Looking for a homey alternative to the Big Island's mega-resorts? You've found it. This family-fun property (the owners live on site) features two cottages set in the foothills of the Kohala Mountains. Cottages are nicely turned out with hardwood floors and French doors; one has a wood-burning fireplace; the other has a whirlpool tub. Nice touches include plush English robes and fresh flowers.

Namakani Paio Cabins

$ 10 cabins
3mi west of Hawaii Volcanoes National Park entrance on Rte. 11, Volcano. 808-967-7321. www.volcanohousehotel.com/cabins.htm.

These simple cabins can sleep four people, and are a great value at just $55 per unit. You get a lot more for your money than you do at the Volcano House Hotel (located in the national park), where a much higher price tag gets you plain-Jane motel-style digs. Cabins (and campsites) are reserved through the Volcano House, where you'll also pick up linens and sleeping bags. Bring your own fleece blanket to ward off the chill. Each cabin comes with a grill, a picnic table and access to the campground's restrooms.

HOTELS: BIG ISLAND

MAUI

Fairmont Kea Lani

$$$$$ 450 rooms

*4100 Wailea Alanui Dr., Wailea.
808-875-4100 or 800-659-4100.
www.fairmont.com.*

Fairmont Kea Lani

Set on Wailea's Polo Beach,
this all-suite-and-villa hotel has
cropped up on numerous "best"
lists. Service is a true art form here,
where valets literally sprint to your
car to open the door for you, and
guests—male and female—are
greeted with fresh leis. It's all about
quiet luxury, from the marble
bathtubs to the pale-on-pale dé-
cor. Each one-bedroom suite has
a living room, master bedroom,
and marble bath; oceanfront villas
have two or three bedrooms, a
kitchen, and a plunge pool. The
hotel is bright white and almost
Grecian, set against the cerulean
blue of sea and sky. At night, the
Kea Lani really sparkles, thanks to
well-placed torch lights. Don't miss
a treatment at the hotel's Spa Kea
Lani *(see p79)*, or a meal at Nick's
Fishmarket *(see p168)*.
The Fairmont's casual, poolside
pizza restaurant is a good option,
too, especially if you're travel-
ing with kids. The hotel offers a
children's program, too.

Four Seasons Resort Maui

$$$$$ 308 rooms

*3900 Wailea Alanui, Wailea.
808-874-8000. www.fourseasons.
com/maui.*

Serenity and luxury are the hall-
marks here, where pool attendants
will spritz you with bottled water
and clean your sunglasses if necessary. They'll also help you find a
lounge chair; none of that pesky
"saving seats" action that plagues
other hotels. Rooms are large and
well-appointed. A sunset dinner at
Ferarro's is not to be missed.

Hotel Hana-Maui

$$$$$ 66 rooms

*5021 Hana Hwy., Hana.
808-248-8211 or 800-321-4262.
www.hotelhanamaui.com.*

Bungalow-style suites and sea
ranch cottages blend into the
landscape here, where Hana Bay
provides a stunning backdrop.
A gentle, New Age spirit pervades
this property (no TVs, clocks, or
morning newspapers) and no
air-conditioning (ceiling fans
do the job). Guest rooms boast
contemporary Hawaiian art, gorgeous shell sconces and wood
countertops, and sweet touches
like a goodie basket and free soda

Hotel Hana-Maui

MUST STAY